Kaplan Keys

ADVANTAGE

Mathematics

GRADE **8**

Kaplan Keys Advantage
Mathematics Grade 8

TOC

Table of Contents

Student Introduction to Kaplan *Keys Advantage*

How to Use This Book

16 Lessons to Learn the Strategies

Each lesson has four parts.

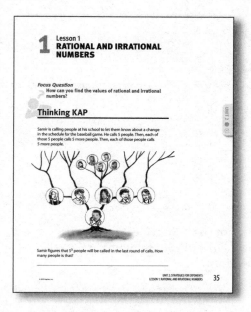

In the Thinking KAP, you will solve a real-world problem about math.

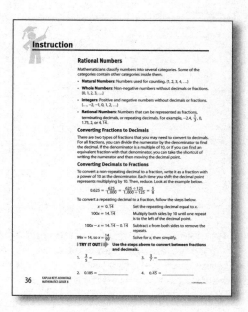

In the Instruction, you will learn new strategies and review important concepts.

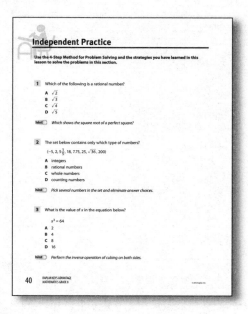

In the Independent Practice, you will use the strategies you have learned to answer questions.

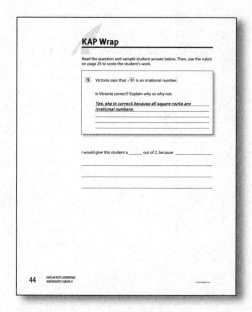

In the KAP Wrap, you will score a sample student response to an open-ended question.

The 4-Step Method for Problem Solving

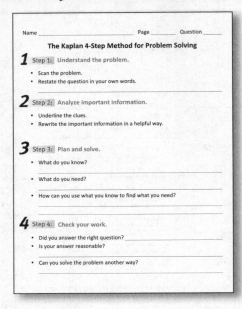

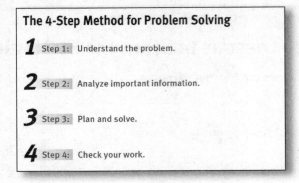

The Kaplan 4-Step Method for math will help you with every problem. You can use the worksheet to write out each step. Ask your teacher for more worksheets when you need them.

Tear out the 4-Step Method reference sheet and keep it in your folder to use on all questions.

Practice Tests and Reflection

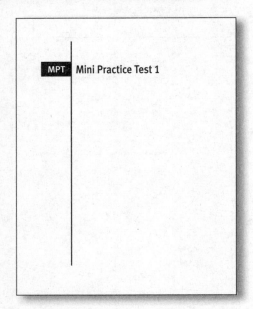

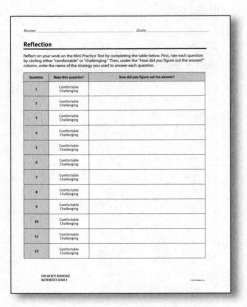

Throughout this program you will also practice using the strategies you have learned by taking Practice Tests. These tests are located online and will be provided by your teacher.

After each Practice Test, you will complete a Reflection. This is your chance to record your thoughts about how easy or difficult each question was for you, and which strategy helped you the most.

Applying the 4-Step Method for Problem Solving

Doing What Great Test-Takers Do

The 4-Step Method for Problem Solving will help you with every question. You can use the worksheet on the next page to write out each step. Ask your teacher for more worksheets when you need them. Tear out the reference sheets and keep them in your folder to use on all questions.

The Kaplan 4-Step Method for Problem Solving

1 Step 1: Understand the problem.

- Scan the problem.
- Restate the question in your own words.

_____

2 Step 2: Analyze important information.

- Underline the clues.
- Rewrite the important information in a helpful way.

3 Step 3: Plan and solve.

- What do you know?

_____

- What do you need?

_____

- How can you use what you know to find what you need?

_____

_____

4 Step 4: Check your work.

- Did you answer the right question? _____
- Is your answer reasonable?

_____

- Can you solve the problem another way?

_____

The Kaplan 4-Step Method for Problem Solving

1 **Step 1:** Understand the problem.

- Scan the problem.
- Restate the question in your own words.

2 **Step 2:** Analyze important information.

- Underline the clues.
- Rewrite the important information in a helpful way.

3 **Step 3:** Plan and solve.

- What do you know?
- What do you need?
- How can you use what you know to find what you need?

4 **Step 4:** Check your work.

- Did you answer the right question?
- Is your answer reasonable?
- Can you solve the problem another way?

The 4-Step Method for Problem Solving

1 **Step 1:** Understand the problem.

2 **Step 2:** Analyze important information.

3 **Step 3:** Plan and solve.

4 **Step 4:** Check your work.

UNIT 1 The 4-Step Method for Problem Solving

1 Lesson 1
GETTING READY

Focus Question

How can you better understand problems before you solve them?

Thinking KAP

Solve both problems below.

1. Solve the equation below for *a*.

   $$3(a - 2) + a = 14$$

   Answer $a =$ _____

2. Aisha bought *a* avocados to make guacamole. Rob bought 3 times 2 less than the number of avocados Aisha bought. The total number of avocados they bought was 14. How many avocados did Aisha buy?

   Answer _____ avocados

What do you notice about problems 1 and 2?

_____

_____

_____

Which problem was more difficult to solve?

_____

_____

_____

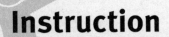

Instruction

Getting Started

Welcome to Kaplan *Keys Advantage*! In each lesson of this program, you will learn strategies for solving problems. The best place to start is by learning a method that can help you with *any* problem—the 4-Step Method for Problem Solving.

The 4-Step Method for Problem Solving will help you understand and work through word problems, so you can solve them more easily.

The 4-Step Method for Problem Solving

1 Step 1: Understand the problem.

2 Step 2: Analyze important information.

3 Step 3: Plan and solve.

4 Step 4: Check your work.

How is the 4-Step Method for Problem Solving like methods you have used before? How is it different?

_____

_____

_____

_____

Understanding the Problem

Before you solve a math problem, you need to figure out what the problem is basically about and what you are being asked to find.

> **1** **Step 1:** Understand the problem.
>
> • Scan the problem.
> • Restate the question in your own words.

Scan the Problem

When you see a math problem, the first thing you should do is quickly read it. As you read, try to get a general sense of what the problem is about. How is this problem like others you have solved before? How is it different?

Restate the Question in Your Own Words

To make sure you understand the problem you are being asked to solve, restate the question in your own words.

┃TRY IT OUT┃➡ **Complete Step 1 for the problem below.**

1 The height of flower A, in inches, can be represented by the expression ($2w + 3$), where w represents the number of weeks since flower A was planted. If flower B is ($3w + 1$) inches tall, how much taller is flower B than flower A in terms of w?

A 〔　　　〕◀- - - - - - - - - - - - - - - - - -
B 〔　　　〕
C 〔　　　〕
D 〔　　　〕

The answer choices have been covered up. Don't solve the problem during Step 1!

What is the problem basically about? _____

_____

Restate the problem in your own words. _____

_____

Analyzing the Important Information

In Step 2, you will read the problem again—this time more carefully. As you read, you will underline the clues.

> **2** Step 2: Analyze important information.
>
> - Underline the clues.
> - Rewrite the important information in a helpful way.

What Is a Clue?

A clue tells you about the math in a problem, not the story. Think of a clue as something that could help you solve the problem.

❚TRY IT OUT❚➡ **Underline the clues in the problem. Then, explain three of the clues on the lines provided.**

1 The height of flower A, in inches, can be represented by the expression $(2w + 3)$, where w represents the number of weeks since flower A was planted. If flower B is $(3w + 1)$ inches tall, how much taller is flower B than flower A in terms of w?

A $2 - w$

B $w - 2$

C $w + 2$

D $w + 4$

The clue _____ *(2w + 3)* _____ tells me *the height of flower A*

in terms of w   .

The clue _____ *(3w + 1)* _____ tells me _____

_____ .

The clue _____ tells me _____

_____ .

Rewriting the Important Information

Draw It

One way to rewrite important information is to draw a simple diagram to help you understand the information you are given. Diagrams are helpful for problems about parts and totals. They are also helpful for many measurement and geometry problems.

Chart It

Another way to organize information is to make a chart. Charts are helpful for problems that involve changes over time, patterns and relationships, and data from surveys or experiments.

▌TRY IT OUT▐ ➡ **Make a diagram or chart to rewrite the important information in the problem on page 6.**

Independent Practice

Use the 4-Step Method for Problem Solving to solve the problems in this section.

1 What is the approximate diameter of a circle with an area of 50.24 square centimeters?

    A 4 centimeters

    B 7 centimeters

    C 8 centimeters

    D 16 centimeters

hint *Draw a diagram to help you organize and analyze the important information.*

2 Which algebraic expression represents "four times the sum of x and five"?

    A $4 + 5x$

    B $4x + 5$

    C $4(x + 5)$

    D $5(4 + x)$

hint *Translate this expression in parts. Each part should include one mathematical operation.*

3 How many U.S. dollars can you get for 252 Mexican pesos if the exchange rate is 10.5 pesos per dollar?

    A $24

    B $25.20

    C $241.50

    D $2,646

hint *Set up a proportion to help you solve this problem.*

4 Which equation **best** describes the functional relationship shown below?

x	y
−2	6
−1	3
0	0
1	−3
2	−6

A $y = -3x$

B $y = x - 3$

C $y = x + 8$

D $y = -2x + 2$

hint *Find a function for which the ordered pair (0,0) is a solution.*

5 Line *m* intersects line ℓ below.

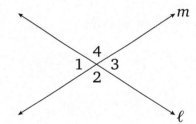

Which two angles are congruent?

A ∠1 and ∠2

B ∠1 and ∠3

C ∠2 and ∠3

D ∠4 and ∠1

hint *Which pairs of angles formed by intersecting lines must be congruent?*

6   What is the measure of angle R in the figure below?

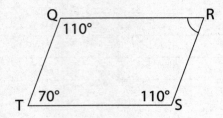

A   55°

B   70°

C   80°

D   250°

hint ▷ *Recall what you know about the sum of the interior angles of a quadrilateral.*

7   Which two whole numbers is $\sqrt{40}$ between?

A   4 and 5

B   6 and 7

C   8 and 9

D   20 and 21

hint ▷ *It may help to make a list of the first 10 perfect squares and their square roots.*

8   Kuoching wrote the following numbers in scientific notation:

$$4.2 \times 10^3, \qquad 8.5 \times 10^2, \qquad 1.7 \times 10^4, \qquad 6.3 \times 10^3$$

Which number written in scientific notation is **greatest**?

A 1.7×10^4

B 4.2×10^3

C 6.3×10^3

D 8.5×10^2

hint ▷ *Compare the exponents first.*

9   What is the best **estimation**, in square millimeters, for the surface area of the right circular cylinder shown below?

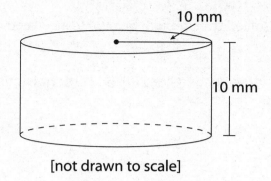

10 mm

10 mm

[not drawn to scale]

$$\text{Surface area} = 2\pi rh + 2\pi r^2$$

A   600 square millimeters

B   900 square millimeters

C   1,200 square millimeters

D   3,100 square millimeters

hint ▷   *Substitute the relevant information from the diagram into the given formula.*

10   In the diagram below, line *m* and line *n* are parallel.

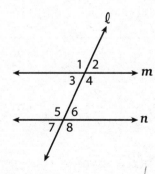

Which of the statements below about angle relationships is **always** true?

A $m\angle 1 + m\angle 2 = 90°$

B $m\angle 5 + m\angle 7 = 90°$

C $\angle 3 \cong \angle 4$

D $\angle 3 \cong \angle 6$

hint ▷   *Think about why it is significant that lines m and n are parallel.*

KAP Wrap

Paolo solved the problem below. He incorrectly answered (D).

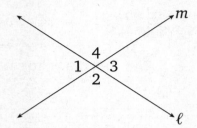

1 Intersecting lines *m* and *l* are shown below.

Which of the following is true?

A Angles 1 and 2 are vertical.

B Angles 1 and 2 are congruent.

C Angles 1 and 2 are supplementary.

D Angles 1 and 2 are complementary.

Describe the error that Paolo made. _____

_____

_____

_____

What is the correct answer? _____

2 Lesson 2
TAKING ACTION

Focus Question

What strategies can you use to solve problems and check your work?

Thinking KAP

Underline the important clues in the problem below.

> Ms. Sullivan is buying her class a set of dry-erase markers and erasers. If markers come in packages of 9 and erasers come in packages of 6, what is the minimum number of packages of markers and erasers she must buy so that each marker has an eraser and there are no leftover markers or erasers?

Restate the question in your own words. _____

_____

_____

Make a chart or diagram to analyze the important information.

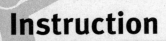

Instruction

Making a Plan

Once you understand a problem, you need to make a plan to solve it. Look back at what the problem asks for and what important information it gives you. Then, decide how to use what you are given to solve the problem.

3 Step 3: Plan and solve.

- What do you know?
- What do you need?
- How can you use what you know to find what you need?

TRY IT OUT **Complete Steps 1 and 2 for the problem below. You will solve the problem on the next page.**

1 Liz, Israel, and Matt all have coin collections. Liz has 7 quarters in hers and Israel has 5 more than twice as many as Matt has. If they have a total of 30 quarters, how many does Matt have?

    A 6

    B 12

    C 18

    D 35

Restate the problem in your own words. _____

_____

Underline the important clues in the problem. Then, draw a diagram or make a chart to help you understand the important information.

▌TRY IT OUT▐ ➡ Now, use the three planning questions from Step 3 to solve the problem on the previous page.

What do you know?

What information is in the problem? _____

_____

_____

What do you need?

What do you need to find in order to solve the problem? _____

_____

_____

How can you use what you know to find what you need?

Describe your plan.

_____

_____

_____

Carry out your plan to solve the problem.

Checking Your Work

The best way to improve your score on any math test is to check your work. To check your work, ask yourself the three questions below.

 Step 4: Check your work.

- Did you answer the right question?
- Is your answer reasonable?
- Can you solve the problem another way?

Did you answer the right question?

One reason students get questions wrong is that they do not answer the question asked in the problem. After you solve a problem, go back to Step 1 and review the question you restated in your own words. Is this the question you answered?

▌TRY IT OUT▐ ➡ **A student solved the problem below incorrectly. Find the mistake.**

1 Liz, Israel, and Matt all have coin collections. Liz has 7 quarters in hers and Israel has 5 more than twice as many as Matt has. If they have a total of 30 quarters, how many does Matt have?

    A 6

    B 12

    (**C**) 18

    D 35

Refer to your calculations from the previous page. What mistake could this student have made to get (C) as an answer?

_____

_____

_____

Is your answer reasonable?

Go back to the information you organized in Step 2. Does your answer make sense when you add it to the diagram or chart you made? Is it reasonable when you compare it to what you already know?

‖ TRY IT OUT ‖ ➡ **A student solved the problem below incorrectly. Find the mistake.**

1 Liz, Israel, and Matt all have coin collections. Liz has 7 quarters in hers and Israel has 5 more than twice as many as Matt has. If they have a total of 30 quarters, how many does Matt have?

    A 6

    B 12

    C 18

    (D) 35

Compare this answer to the total number of quarters the three friends have. Why is this answer unreasonable?

_____

_____

_____

_____

Can you solve the problem another way?

In Step 3, you planned a problem-solving strategy and carried out your plan. Solving the problem another way can help you convince yourself that your answer is correct. If you solve the problem another way and don't get the same answer, check both of your computations.

In the space below, solve the above problem another way.

Independent Practice

Use the 4-Step Method for Problem Solving to solve the problems in this section.

1 Angle A is complementary to angle B. If angle A measures 28°, what is the measure of angle B?

    A 28°

    B 62°

    C 128°

    D 152°

hint ▷ *Draw and label a diagram to help you visualize the angles.*

2 Leon bought a pack of 6 guitar strings for $8.34. How much did he pay per string?

    A $1.00

    B $1.39

    C $2.34

    D $50.04

hint ▷ *The phrase "per string" indicates that you must calculate the unit rate.*

3 Between what two whole numbers is $\sqrt{78}$?

    A 7 and 8

    B 8 and 9

    C 9 and 10

    D 39 and 40

hint ▷ *It may help to make a list of the first ten perfect squares and their square roots.*

4 The population of India is approximately 1,130,000,000 people. What is this number expressed in scientific notation?

A 113×10^3

B 11.3×10^5

C 1.13×10^6

D 1.13×10^9

UNIT 1 ① ③

hint *It may help to write each answer choice in standard form.*

5 In the diagram below, $\overleftrightarrow{AB}$ intersects $\overleftrightarrow{CE}$ at point D, and the measure of $\angle EDB$ is 35°.

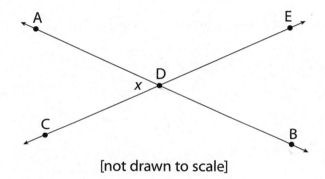

[not drawn to scale]

What is the measure, in degrees, of $\angle x$?

A 35°

B 55°

C 145°

D 325°

hint *Recall the special relationship between vertical angles.*

6 Which situation is best represented by the expression 10s + 25?

    A Carolyn starts jogging 25 feet from her house and jogs 10 feet per second.

    B Carolyn jogs 10 feet per second for 25 seconds.

    C Carolyn jogs 10 feet every 25 seconds.

    D Carolyn jogs for 10 seconds and rests for 25 seconds.

hint   *Pay attention to the operations in the algebraic expression: multiplication and addition.*

7 Which of the graphs below shows a linear relationship?

A

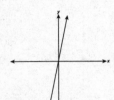

C

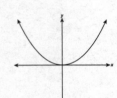

B

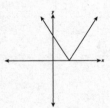

D

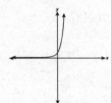

hint   *Linear sounds like the word line. Which graph shows this relationship?*

8 Which equation best describes the functional relationship shown below?

x	y
−2	2
−1	3
0	4
1	5
2	6

A $y = -2x$

B $y = 3x$

C $y = x + 1$

D $y = x + 4$

hint ▷ *Find a function for which the ordered pair (0, 4) is a solution.*

9 Lily wrote the following equation on the board.

$$y = 3x - 4$$

Which table shows the pattern from Lily's equation?

A

x	−1	0	1	2
y	1	−4	0	5

B

x	−1	0	1	2
y	1	−4	7	10

C

x	−1	0	1	2
y	−7	0	2	4

D

x	−1	0	1	2
y	−7	−4	−1	2

hint ▷ *Substitute each input value for x to find the y values.*

KAP Wrap

Jeannine solved the problem below. She incorrectly answered (A).

---

1   Robyn's Boutique adds a 25% markup to all clothing it buys
before reselling it. For how much would the store sell a jacket
it bought for $60?

(A) $15

B $25

C $75

D $85

Describe the error Jeannine made. _____

_____

_____

_____

What is the correct answer? _____

3 Lesson 3
OPEN-ENDED PROBLEMS

Focus Question

What do you need to do to earn full credit for open-ended problems?

Thinking KAP

Read the sample student work and thinking below. Label where the student completed each step of the 4-Step Method for Problem Solving.

1   Romero went to the batting cages and hit <u>9 out of 12</u> pitches. If the <u>ratio</u> of hits to total pitches <u>stays the same</u>, how many hits could he expect out of <u>20 pitches</u>?

A   9

B   12

C   15

D   17

Instruction

Open-Ended Problems

Open-ended problems do not have answer choices. They may also ask you to show your work and explain your answer.

Some open-ended problems are worth three points. The rubric below shows how test graders score three-point problems.

3-Point Response	You show that you really understand the problem. You show all your work, and the work is all correct. You clearly explain how you solved the problem.
2-Point Response	You show that you mostly understand the problem. You show all your work, and the work is almost all correct. You explain how you solved the problem, but your explanation might not be clear.
1-Point Response	You show that you understand some of the problem. You show some of your work, but the work might have some big mistakes in it. You don't completely explain how you solved the problem.
0-Point Response	You show that you don't understand the problem. You might not show any work. If you do show work, you made a lot of mistakes. You don't explain how you solved the problem.

Think of the rubric this way:

- You get one point for a correct answer.
- You get one point for showing correct work when asked.
- You get one point for explaining your work when asked.

Short-Response Problems

Shorter problems will be worth only two points. The rubric below shows how test graders score two-point problems.

2-Point Response	You show that you really understand the problem. You show all your work, and the work is all correct. You clearly explain how you solved the problem.
1-Point Response	You show that you understand some of the problem. You provide a correct answer but do not show your work or explain your steps.
0-Point Response	You show that you don't understand the problem. You might not show any work. If you do show work, it has a lot of mistakes. You don't explain how you solved the problem.

▌TRY IT OUT▌➡ **Use the rubric above to score the sample student work below.**

2 Maria has a plastic container with a 4-gallon capacity. She puts 10 pints of punch in the container.

How many gallons of punch are in Maria's container?

Show your work.

10 pints = 1.25 gallons

Answer ___1.25___ gallons

I would give this student a _____ out of 2, because _____

_____.

Say It! Support It!

Use the strategy below to make sure you earn the highest possible score for open-ended problems.

Say it! Support it!
• **Say it!**　　Write your answer.
• **Support it!**　Show and explain your thinking so that someone else can understand it.

▌TRY IT OUT▐ ➡　　**Use Say it! Support it! to solve the problem below.**

3　Sam is building a square picture frame, and needs to determine the length of each side. He knows the area enclosed by the frame will be 80 square centimeters.

Between which two whole numbers is $\sqrt{80}$?

Show your work.

Support your answer here.

Say your answer here.

Answer _____ and _____

On the lines below, explain how you arrived at your answer.

Support your answer here.

_____

_____

_____

Use Say it! Support it! to show your work for the problem below.

4   In the diagram below, lines *e* and *f* intersect. What is the measure of ∠*g*?

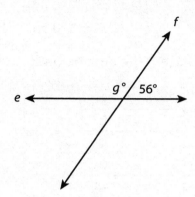

Show your work.

Answer _____

On the lines below, explain how you determined your answer.

_____

_____

_____

_____

_____

Use the questions below to look back at your answer.

☐   My answer is correct.

☐   My work helps the reader understand how I got the answer.

☐   My explanation is clear even to someone who doesn't know me.

Independent Practice

Use the 4-Step Method for Problem Solving and the strategies you have learned in this lesson to solve the problems in this section.

1 Write an algebraic function that could represent the data below.

x	y
−2	8
−1	4
0	0
1	−4
2	−8

Show your work.

Answer $y =$ _____

hint *Think carefully about what the y-value at x = 0 tells you about the operation in this function.*

2 Solve the equation below for *b*.

$$2(b - 5) = 4b + 8$$

Show your work.

$$2b - 10 = 4b + 8$$
$$\underline{-4b \qquad -4b}$$
$$-2b - 10 = 8$$
$$\underline{+10 \quad +10}$$
$$\frac{-2b}{-2} = \frac{18}{-2}$$

Answer _____−9_____

hint *Remember what happens to negative and positive numbers when they are divided by negative numbers.*

3 A right circular cylinder is shown below.

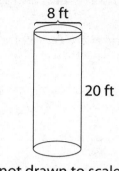

8 ft

20 ft

[not drawn to scale]

Calculate the volume of the cylinder above. Use 3.14 to approximate π.

$$V = \pi r^2 h$$

Show your work.

$V = 3.14 (4^2) 20$

$V = 3.14 (16) 20$

$V = 3.14 (320)$

$V =$

$\begin{array}{r} 20 \\ \times 16 \\ \hline 120 \\ 20 \\ \hline 320 \end{array}$

$\begin{array}{r} 320 \\ \times 3.14 \\ \hline 1280 \\ 320 \\ 960 \\ \hline 1004.80 \end{array}$

Answer _____ cubic feet

On the lines below, explain how you arrived at your answer.

_____

_____

_____

hint ▷ *Check your work to be sure you substituted the correct values into the formula.*

4 In the diagram below, line *a* and line *b* are parallel.

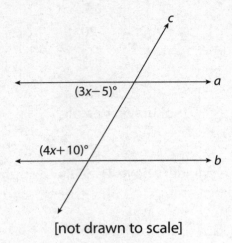

$(3x-5)°$

$(4x+10)°$

[not drawn to scale]

Solve for *x*.

Show your work.

Answer $x =$ _____

hint ▷ *Use the relationships between interior angles to set up an equation.*

5 At Lee's local bodega, mangoes are on sale today. Lee can get 5 mangoes for $3. How much would it cost to buy 3 mangoes?

Show your work.

Answer $ _____

hint ▷ *One way to approach this problem is to set up a proportion to calculate the unit rate.*

6   A tank holding water is draining at a constant rate of 5 gallons per minute. When you begin measuring the volume at time $t = 0$, it contains 55 gallons of water.

Complete the table of values below based on this scenario.

Time, t, in minutes	Volume, V, in gallons
0	55
1	50
2	45

Write an algebraic function that could represent the data above.

Answer $y =$ _____

On the lines below, explain how you determined your answer.

_____

_____

_____

_____

_____

hint   *Determine the rate of change from the table of values and use this and the value of the volume at $t = 0$ to help you determine the equation of this function.*

KAP Wrap

Read the question and sample student answer below. Then, use the rubric on page 25 to score the student's work.

---

1 Carson ordered five rational numbers from least to greatest as shown below:

$$-\frac{7}{8}, \frac{1}{3}, \frac{2}{9}, \frac{3}{5}, \frac{4}{7}$$

Is Carson correct? Explain your answer below.

No, Carson is not correct. She understood that the negative number had the least value, but she ordered all other rational numbers by the value of their numerators without considering their denominators. The correct order is $-\frac{7}{8}, \frac{2}{9}, \frac{1}{3}, \frac{4}{7}, \frac{3}{5}.$

I would give this student a _____ out of 2, because _____

_____

_____

_____

UNIT 2 Strategies for Exponents

1

Lesson 1
RATIONAL AND IRRATIONAL NUMBERS

Focus Question
How can you find the values of rational and irrational numbers?

Thinking KAP

Samir is calling people at his school to let them know about a change in the schedule for the baseball game. He calls 5 people. Then, each of those 5 people calls 5 more people. Then, each of those people calls 5 more people.

Samir figures that 5^3 people will be called in the last round of calls. How many people is that?

125 people

Rational Numbers

Mathematicians classify numbers into several categories. Some of the categories contain other categories inside them.

- **Natural Numbers**: Numbers used for counting. {1, 2, 3, 4, ...}
- **Whole Numbers**: Non-negative numbers without decimals or fractions. {0, 1, 2, 3, ...}
- **Integers**: Positive and negative numbers without decimals or fractions. {..., −2, −1, 0, 1, 2, ...}
- **Rational Numbers**: Numbers that can be represented as fractions, terminating decimals, or repeating decimals. For example, −2.4, $\frac{1}{3}$, 0, 1.75, 2, or $4.\overline{14}$.

Converting Fractions to Decimals

There are two types of fractions that you may need to convert to decimals. For all fractions, you can divide the numerator by the denominator to find the decimal. If the denominator is a multiple of 10, or if you can find an equivalent fraction with that denominator, you can take the shortcut of writing the numerator and then moving the decimal point.

Converting Decimals to Fractions

To convert a non-repeating decimal to a fraction, write it as a fraction with a power of 10 as the denominator. Each time you shift the decimal point represents multiplying by 10. Then, reduce. Look at the example below.

$$0.625 = \frac{625}{1,000} = \frac{625 \div 125}{1,000 \div 125} = \frac{5}{8}$$

To convert a repeating decimal to a fraction, follow the steps below.

$x = 0.\overline{14}$	Set the repeating decimal equal to x.
$100x = 14.\overline{14}$	Multiply both sides by 10 until one repeat is to the left of the decimal point.
$100x - x = 14.\overline{14} - 0.\overline{14}$	Subtract x from both sides to remove the repeats.
$99x = 14$, so $x = \frac{14}{99}$	Solve for x, then simplify.

▌TRY IT OUT▐➡ **Use the steps above to convert between fractions and decimals.**

1. $\frac{3}{5} =$ _0.60_

2. $0.185 =$ _$\frac{185}{999}$_

3. $\frac{3}{7} =$ _0.428753_

4. $0.\overline{45} =$ _$\frac{45}{99}$_

(handwritten long division work in left margin:)

42.8
7)300
  28
  20
  14
  60
  56
  40

$\frac{3}{7} = \frac{x}{100}$

Squares and Cubes

Imagine a line with length 2. If you use that measurement to make a square, its area will be 2 × 2 or "2 squared," which is written as 2^2. If you use the measurement to make a cube, its volume will be 2 × 2 × 2 or "2 cubed," which is written as 2^3. You can also say "two to the third" or "two to the third power."

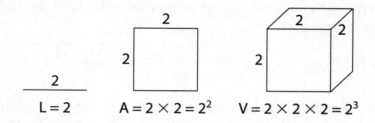

L = 2   A = 2 × 2 = 2^2 V = 2 × 2 × 2 = 2^3

Perfect Squares and Perfect Cubes

When a whole number is squared or cubed, the product is called a perfect square or perfect cube. You should memorize all of the perfect squares up to 15^2 and perfect cubes up to 4^3.

❚TRY IT OUT❚➡ **Complete the table. Circle relationships you need to memorize.**

$0^2 =$ 0	$7^2 =$ 44	$14^2 =$
$1^2 =$ 1	$8^2 =$ 64	$15^2 =$
$2^2 =$ 4	$9^2 =$ 81	$0^3 =$
$3^2 =$ 9	$10^2 =$ 100	$1^3 =$
$4^2 =$ 16	$11^2 =$ 128	$2^3 =$
$5^2 =$ 25	$12^2 =$	$3^3 =$
$6^2 =$ 36	$13^2 =$	$4^3 =$

Classify each of the following numbers as perfect squares, perfect cubes, both, or neither.

1. 100 ___Perfect square___
2. 50 ___Niether___
3. 25 ___Perfect square___
4. 88 ___Niether___
5. 27 ___Perfect cube___
6. 0 ___~~Niether~~ Both___
7. 121 ___Perfect square___
8. 64 ___Both___

Square Roots

A square root is the number which, when multiplied by itself, has the product given under the square root sign. You can find the square root of a perfect square by memorizing the relationship. The same works for cube roots. For example,

$$\sqrt{25} = 5 \qquad \sqrt{196} = \underline{14} \qquad \sqrt[3]{8} = \underline{2}$$

Most whole numbers, however, do not have whole numbers for their square roots. To find the square root of these numbers, first think of the two perfect squares the number is between. Then, use guess-and-check to test each digit. For example, what is the square root of 27, to the nearest hundredth?

27 is between 25 and 36, so $\sqrt{27}$ is between 5 and 6.

Guess 5.5: $5.5^2 = 30.25$. This is too big. Try something smaller.

Guess 5.2: $5.2^2 = 27.04$. This is almost perfect. Try something a bit smaller.

Guess 5.19: $5.19^2 = 26.9361$. This is farther away.

To the nearest hundredth, $\sqrt{27} = 5.20$.

Estimation versus Exact Answers

When you represent an irrational number with a decimal expansion, the decimal is always an estimate, no matter how many decimal places you show. When you write open-ended answers, always keep your answers in terms of π or a square root unless the problem asks you to estimate.

▌TRY IT OUT ▌➤ **Find the square or cube root of each number below. Round decimals to the nearest hundredth.**

1. $\sqrt{54} =$ _____

2. $\sqrt{81} =$ _____

3. $\sqrt[3]{0} =$ _____

4. $\sqrt{7} =$ _____

Irrational Numbers and Inverse Operations

As you have seen, all decimals that terminate or repeat can be written as ratios. However, **irrational numbers** never terminate or repeat. For example, π continues forever without repeating.

$$\pi = 3.14159265358979323846264338327950288419716939937510...$$

Irrational Numbers and Square Roots

All square roots of integers that are not perfect squares are irrational. Their decimal representations go on forever without repeating and they cannot be written as ratios.

$$\sqrt{1} = 1$$

$$\sqrt{2} = 1.41421356237309504880168872420969807856967187537694...$$

$$\sqrt{3} = 1.73205080756887729352744634150587236694280525381038...$$

$$\sqrt{4} = 2$$

$$\sqrt{5} = 2.23606797749978969640917366873127623544061835961152...$$

Inverse Operations

The square and cube operations are **inverses** of the root operations. Inverse operations "undo" each other. Notice how the inverse operations can be used to simplify in the examples below.

$$x^3 = 27 \qquad\qquad \sqrt{y} = 15$$

$$\sqrt[3]{x^3} = \sqrt[3]{27} \qquad\qquad \left(\sqrt{y}\right)^2 = 15^2$$

$$x = 3 \qquad\qquad y = 255$$

ⅠTRY IT OUTⅠ ➡ **Solve the problems below.**

1 Which number is an irrational number?

A $-\dfrac{9}{7}$ **C** $2.\overline{6}$

B $\sqrt{49}$ **D** $\sqrt{20}$

2 Place each value on the number line below.

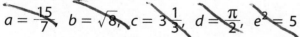

$a = \dfrac{15}{7}, \quad b = \sqrt{8}, \quad c = 3\dfrac{1}{3}, \quad d = \dfrac{\pi}{2}, \quad e^2 = 5$

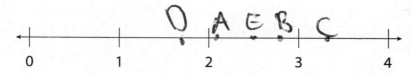

Independent Practice

Use the 4-Step Method for Problem Solving and the strategies you have learned in this lesson to solve the problems in this section.

1   Which of the following is a rational number?

   A $\sqrt{2}$

   B $\sqrt{3}$

   C $\sqrt{4}$

   D $\sqrt{5}$

hint   *Which shows the square root of a perfect square?*

2   The set below contains only which type of numbers?

   $(-5, 2, 5\frac{1}{5}, 18, 7.75, 25, \sqrt{36}, 200)$

   A   integers

   B   rational numbers

   C   whole numbers

   D   counting numbers

hint   *Pick several numbers in the set and eliminate answer choices.*

3   What is the value of *x* in the equation below?

   $x^3 = 64$

   A   2

   B   4

   C   8

   D   16

hint   *Perform the inverse operation of cubing on both sides.*

4 Which of the following describes irrational numbers?

    A terminating decimals

    B repeating decimals

    C repeating, non-terminating decimals

    D non-repeating, non-terminating decimals

hint *Choose a number to represent each choice. Which is irrational?*

5 Between which two whole numbers is $\sqrt{70}$?

    A 5 and 6

    B 6 and 7

    C 7 and 8

    D 8 and 9

hint *Square each number in the answer choices and eliminate.*

6 Which number is an irrational number?

    A $\sqrt{9}$

    B $\sqrt{21}$

    C $\sqrt{49}$

    D $\sqrt{121}$

hint *Which number under the square root symbol is not a perfect square?*

7 Find the value of *a* in the equation below.

$$\sqrt{a} = 14$$

    A 144

    B 169

    C 196

    D 225

hint *What is the inverse operation of taking a square root?*

8 Mr. Williams wrote the following numbers on the board.

$$1.7, \sqrt{8}, 3.\overline{3}, \frac{15}{7}, \sqrt{2}, \frac{7}{8}, \pi, \sqrt{0}$$

Place the numbers in their approximate locations on the number line below. Label each number.

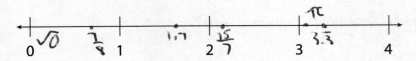

Show your work.

hint ▷ *Convert all the numbers to decimals first.*

9 Find the value of m in the expression below to the nearest hundredth.

$$m^2 = 40$$

Show your work.

Answer <u>Between 6 and 7</u>

hint ▷ Which two perfect squares is 40 between?

KAP Wrap

Read the question and sample student answer below. Then, use the rubric on page 25 to score the student's work.

---

1 Victoria says that $\sqrt{81}$ is an irrational number.

Is Victoria correct? Explain why or why not.

Yes, she is correct because all square roots are irrational numbers.

I would give this student a __O__ out of 2, because __$\sqrt{81}$__ is a rational number it terminates

2 Lesson 2
OPERATIONS WITH EXPONENTS AND SCIENTIFIC NOTATION

Focus Question

How can you work with numbers in exponential form?

Thinking KAP

Anita is cutting a large piece of paper into small squares to make cards for her friends. She cuts the paper in two. Then, she puts the two halves on top of each other and cuts them in half again. She repeats this 5 times.

What exponential expression shows how many pieces of paper she has after 5 cuts?

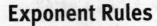
Exponent Rules

You know that an exponent represents repeated multiplication.

$$7^4 = 7 \times 7 \times 7 \times 7 \qquad 8^3 = \underline{8} \times \underline{8} \times \underline{8}$$

You may be asked to simplify exponential expressions that use multiplication and division. As long as the expressions have the same base, you can simplify by expanding.

Multiplication

To simplify an expression like $5^4 \times 5^2$, expand the expression first.

$$5^4 \times 5^2 = (5 \times 5 \times 5 \times 5) \times (5 \times 5) = 5^6$$

You can also take a shortcut: add the exponents. However, if you forget the shortcut, expand the expression. If you use the shortcut, don't forget to expand the expression to check your answer.

Division

To simplify an expression like $6^7 \div 6^3$, expand the expression first.

$$6^7 \div 6^3 = \frac{6 \cdot 6 \cdot 6 \cdot 6 \cdot \cancel{6} \cdot \cancel{6} \cdot \cancel{6}}{\cancel{6} \cdot \cancel{6} \cdot \cancel{6}} = 6^4$$

You can also take a shortcut: subtract the exponents. Again, if you forget the shortcut, expand the expression.

▌TRY IT OUT▐➤ **Use exponent rules to simplify each exponent. If an expression cannot be simplified, write NO.**

1. $4^5 \times 4^2 =$ _____ 4^7

2. $8^5 \times 7^2 =$ _____ NO

3. $7^4 \times 7^5 =$ _____ 7^9

4. $5^6 \div 5^2 =$ _____ 5^4

5. $3^5 \div 3^4 =$ _____ 3^1

6. $2^6 \times 9^5 =$ _____ NO

Negative Exponents and Zero Exponents

Negative exponents are used to show the multiplicative inverse of positive exponents. For example:

$$2^{-3} = \frac{1}{2^3}$$

Because multiplication and division are inverse operations, multiplying by 1 over a number is the same as dividing by that number.

$$10^4 \times 10^{-6} = \frac{10 \cdot 10 \cdot 10 \cdot 10}{10 \cdot 10 \cdot 10 \cdot 10 \cdot 10 \cdot 10} = \frac{1}{10} \times \frac{1}{10} = \frac{1}{100}$$

How can you write $\frac{1}{100}$, with exponents? _____

If you apply the exponent rule for dividing expressions with the same base, you get this:

$$10^4 \div 10^6 = 10^{(4-6)} = 10^{-2}$$

10^{-2} is equal to all the equivalent values below:

$$10^{-2} = \frac{1}{10^2} = \frac{1}{100} = 0.01$$

Zero Exponents

Now, look at what happens when you divide $10^4 \div 10^4$.

$$10^4 \div 10^4 = \frac{10 \cdot 10 \cdot 10 \cdot 10}{10 \cdot 10 \cdot 10 \cdot 10}$$

If the numerator and denominator of a fraction are equal, what is the value of the fraction?

_____ 1 _____

If you apply the exponent rule for dividing expressions with the same base, you get this:

$$10^4 \div 10^4 = 10^{(4-4)} = 10^0$$

For this reason, any number raised to a power of 0 has a value of 1.

▌TRY IT OUT ▐▶   Answer the question below.

Which expression has the **least** value? Explain how you know.

$$10^4 \div 10^7 \qquad 10^7 \div 10^4 \qquad 10^7 \div 10^7$$

_____

_____

_____

Scientific Notation

Scientific notation is a way of writing numbers that tend to be very large or very small. Every number written in scientific notation has two parts: a *coefficient* greater than or equal to 1 and less than 10, and a power of 10.

To convert a number in standard form into scientific notation, place your pencil on the decimal point. Then, shift your pencil one digit at a time until there is only one non-zero number to the left of the decimal. The number of shifts determines the value of the exponent.

Positive Exponents for Large Numbers

If you shift the decimal point to the left, the exponent is positive.

$$410,000 = 4.1 \times 10^5$$

Negative Exponents for Small Numbers

If you shift the decimal point to the right, the exponent is negative.

$$0.000041 = 4.1 \times 10^{-5}$$

To convert a number in scientific notation into standard form, reverse the process. Move the decimal point the same number of places as the exponent of the 10. For positive exponents, shift the decimal to the right. For negative exponents, shift the decimal to the left.

▌TRY IT OUT▐ ➡ Solve the problems below.

Convert the numbers below to standard form.

1. 4.32×10^6 _____

2. 8.7×10^4 _____

3. 1.9×10^{-5} _____

4. 5.698×10^{-3} _____

Convert the numbers below to scientific notation.

5. 0.00076 _____

6. 0.0907 _____

7. 80,000,000 _____

8. 730,000 _____

© 2013 Kaplan, Inc.

Operations in Scientific Notation

To add or subtract in scientific notation, you must first convert both numbers to the same power of ten. Try $5 \times 10^{12} - 8.4 \times 10^9$ below.

Write 8.4×10^9 with a whole number coefficient. _____

Write 5×10^{12} with the same power of 10. _____

Subtract. _____ Convert to scientific notation. _____

To multiply or divide in scientific notation, multiply or divide the bases and the powers of 10 separately. Remember that in multiplying you **add** the exponents. Try $(5.5 \times 10^{-5}) \times (3.0 \times 10^{-2})$ below.

Multiply: $5.5 \times 3.0 =$ _____ Multiply: $10^{-5} \times 10^{-2} =$ _____

Convert back to scientific notation. _____

Estimating Differences of Scale

A **scale** question will ask you how many times larger or smaller one number is than another. To estimate, use multiplication or division to find the correct power of 10, then estimate with the coefficients. For example:

The diameter of the sun is 1.391×10^6 kilometers. The diameter of Mars is 6.794×10^3 kilometers. How many times greater is the diameter of the sun than the diameter of Mars?

How many times greater is 10^6 than 10^3? _____

Round to find a scalar relationship between 1.391 and 6.794: $1.4 \div 7 = 0.2$.

Multiply the base and the exponent: $0.2 \times 1,000 =$ _____

The sun's diameter is about _____ times greater than Mars'.

▌TRY IT OUT▐ ➡ Solve the problems below.

1. $6.1 \times 10^{-5} + 2.3 \times 10^{-4} =$ _____ 2.91×10^{-4}

2. $(1.1 \times 10^6) \times (7.5 \times 10^3) =$ _____

3. 4.2×10^3 is about _____ times greater than 1.91×10^{-2}.

4. 5.3×10^{-3} is about _____ times greater than 9.2×10^{-5}.

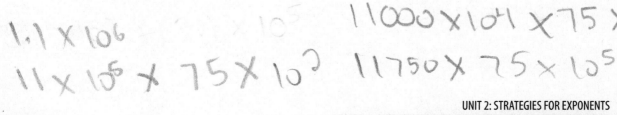

Independent Practice

Use the 4-Step Method for Problem Solving and the strategies you have learned in this lesson to solve the problems in this section.

1 A scientist measured the weight of a substance as 0.000002045 milligrams. How is this number expressed in scientific notation?

   A 20.45×10^{-7}

   B 2.045×10^{-6}

   C 2.045×10^{6}

   D 20.45×10^{7}

hint   *For a very small number, should the exponent be positive or negative?*

2 The distance between two objects is 4.23×10^{7} miles. How is this number written in standard form?

   A 4,230,000

   B 42,300,000

   C 423,000,000

   D 4,230,000,000

hint   *Count the number of places the decimal shifts.*

3 Which of the following expressions is *not* equivalent to $\frac{1}{64}$?

   A $8^{-4} \times 8^{2}$

   B $8^{5} \times 8^{-3}$

   C $8^{-1} \times 8^{-1}$

   D 8×8^{-3}

hint   *If you forget how to multiply numbers with exponents, try writing each one out with multiplication.*

KAPLAN KEYS ADVANTAGE
MATHEMATICS GRADE 8

© 2013 Kaplan, Inc.

4 Carrie wrote the four numbers below in scientific notation.

$$6.2 \times 10^6, \qquad 1.9 \times 10^7, \qquad 3.1 \times 10^6, \qquad 2.1 \times 10^7$$

Which number has the **least** value?

A 6.2×10^6

B 1.9×10^7

C 3.1×10^6

D 2.1×10^7

 hint *First, compare the powers of 10. Then, compare the bases.*

5 A scientist measured the length of a particular bacterium as 3.2×10^{-8} centimeters. What is the number expressed in standard form?

A 0.0000000032

B 0.000000032

C 320,000,000

D 3,200,000,000

hint *Should the number be very large or very small?*

6 Simplify the expression below.

$$3a^6 \cdot a^2$$

A $3a^3$

B $3a^4$

C $3a^8$

D $3a^{12}$

hint *You can multiply in any order. Think of this as $3 \cdot (a^6 \cdot a^2)$*

7 The population of Asia is approximately 3.879×10^9 people. The population of New York state is approximately 1.89×10^7 people.

About how many times greater is the population of Asia than the population of New York state?

A 10 times greater

B 20 times greater

C 100 times greater

D 200 times greater

hint *Round the coefficients to make it easier to compare.*

8 Simplify the expression below.

$$\frac{k^{12}}{k^4}$$

A k^3

B k^8

C k^{16}

D k^{48}

hint *Expand the expression in the numerator and the expression in the denominator.*

9 Red blood cells are around 7×10^{-6} meters. Lindsey is about 1.5 meters tall. About how many times taller is Lindsey than one of her red blood cells?

A 2×10^{-6} times taller

B 2×10^{-5} times taller

C 2×10^5 times taller

D 2×10^6 times taller

hint *Write the size of a red blood cell in standard form.*

10 Priya is trying to find all of the different ways that she can write the product of the two numbers below.

$$2^3 \times 2^{-7}$$

Circle **all** of the numbers or expressions that have the same value as Priya's expression.

2^4 $\quad\quad$ $2^{(3+7)}$ $\quad\quad$ $\dfrac{1}{16}$ $\quad\quad$ 2^{-10} $\quad\quad$ $\dfrac{1}{2^4}$ $\quad\quad$ 8

2^{-4} $\quad\quad$ $\dfrac{1}{2^{-10}}$ $\quad\quad$ 2^{-21} $\quad\quad$ $\dfrac{2^3}{2^{-7}}$ $\quad\quad$ $2^{(3 \times -7)}$

$\dfrac{1}{2^{10}}$ $\quad\quad$ $\dfrac{2^3}{2^7}$ $\quad\quad$ $\dfrac{1}{1,024}$ $\quad\quad$ $\dfrac{1}{8}$ $\quad\quad$ $\dfrac{2^7}{2^3}$

1,024 $\quad\quad$ 2^{10} $\quad\quad$ 16 $\quad\quad$ $\dfrac{1}{2^{-4}}$ $\quad\quad$ $2^{(3-7)}$

On the lines below, explain how you know that the numbers you circled have the same value as the expression.

_____

_____

_____

_____

11 The light travels 0.36 meters in 1.2×10^{-9} seconds. How many meters does it travel in one hour? Express your answer in scientific notation.

Show your work.

Answer _____ meters

KAP Wrap

Read the question and sample student answer below. Then, use the rubric on page 25 to score the student's work.

---

1 Write 0.00009872 in scientific notation.

Answer 9.872×10^5

Explain how you determined your answer.

I moved the decimal point so the first number was greater than 1 and less than 10. Then, I counted how many times I moved the decimal point and wrote that number as the exponent.

I would give this student a _____ out of 2, because _____

_____

_____

_____

UNIT 3 Strategies for Expressions and Equations

Lesson 1
FUNCTIONS

Focus Question

? **How can you show an input-output relationship with equations, graphs, tables, and words?**

Thinking KAP

Leanna is making a map to show the shortest path between her house and her school. Her house is located at (1, 0). Her school is located at (5, 4).

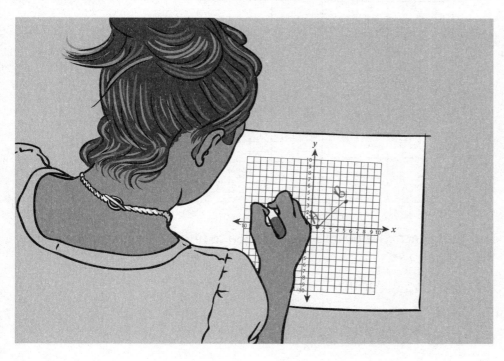

A= House
B= School

Plot the points on Leanna's coordinate grid. Then, draw a line to show the shortest path between the two points.

Name a different point that is on the line. _(3, 2)_

Functions

A **function** is a rule that assigns each input to exactly one output. Functions can be shown as graphs, tables of ordered pairs, equations, or written descriptions.

To use an equation to create a table or graph, choose an input value for x, then substitute it into the equation to find the output value, y.

❚ TRY IT OUT ❚➡ **Solve the problem below.**

1 Complete the table of values for the equation $y = 2x - 1$. Then, use the table of values to graph the line of the equation on the coordinate plane.

x	y
−1	−3
0	−1
1	1
2	3

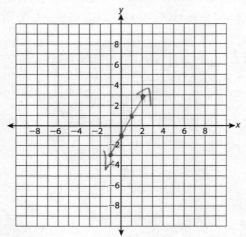

Substitute each x-value into the equation to find each y-value. Then, fill in the table above.

$x = -1;$ $y = 2(-1) - 1 = -3$ $(1, -3)$

$x = $ $y = 2(0) - 1 = 0 - 1 = -1$

$x = $ $y = 2(1) - 1 = 2 - 1 = 1$

$x = $ $y = 2(2) - 1 = 4 - 1 = 3$

Plot the points on the grid above and connect the points to make a line.

Function Notation

Function notation is another way of showing an input-output relationship. When *x* is the input, instead of using *y* as the output, functions notation calls the output **f(x)**, which is read aloud as "*f* of *x*". Function notation can be used with any variables, and in equations and tables. Complete the function table below.

$h(v) = -3v + 2$	**v**	0	1	2
	h(v)	2		

Testing Points

Function equations are used to generate points using the input *x* and the output *y*. To determine whether a point or table matches an equation, substitute the *x*-value for *x* and the *y*-value for *y* for each point.

Remember that **two points** are required to determine a line, so when you compare a table to an equation or graph, you should always test at least two ordered pairs.

▌TRY IT OUT▌➡ **Test points to solve the problems below.**

2 Which equation represents the rule for the values in the table below?

x	**f(x)**
1	5
2	7
3	9

   A $f(x) = x + 4$

   B $f(x) = 3x - 1$

   C $f(x) = 2x + 3$

   D $f(x) = 4x - 3$

3 Which ordered pair is included on the graph of the line $g(x) = 2x + 8$?

   A (8, 0)

   B (8, 1)

   C (1, 8)

   D (0, 8)

Test the point in each answer choice. Eliminate those that do not yield true statements.

Check Your Work

It's easy to make a careless error when graphing lines. You can check that you graphed the correct line by testing points.

- Choose a point on the line.

- Test the point in the equation to check that it makes the equation true.

▌TRY IT OUT▐ ➡ **Test a point to solve the problem below.**

Determine whether the graph below matches the equation $y = x + 5$.

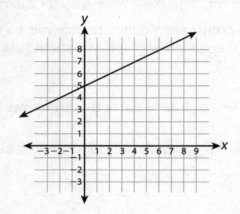

Choose a point on the graph. Try (0, 5). Test this point in the equation.

$$5 \overset{?}{=} 0 + 5 \qquad 5 = 5 \qquad \text{This point satisfies the equation.}$$

Choose another point on the graph. Test this point in the equation.

Your point: (2,6)

Does this point satisfy the equation? No

Is the equation correctly graphed? No   Explain how you know.

_____

_____

Functions and Relations

A **relation** is any rule between inputs and outputs. A **function** is a special type of relation where each input, *x*, has exactly one output, *y*.

The **vertical line test** can be used to determine if a relation is also a function. If you can draw a vertical line that intersects two points on the graph, the graph must have two outputs for the same input. Thus, it is not a function.

❚TRY IT OUT❚ ➡ **Determine whether each relation is a function.**

1.

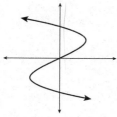

no

3. $h(x) = x + 3$

yes

2.

x	0	1	2	3
f(x)	2	1	2	1

yes

4.

x	2	1	2	1
f(x)	0	1	2	3

no

A **linear function** is a function that makes a line on a graph. Other relationships are **non-linear**.

❚TRY IT OUT❚ ➡ **Graph each equation below. Label each function as linear or non-linear.**

5. $y = -2x$

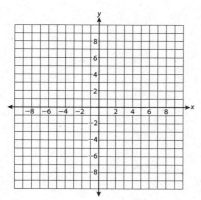

_____

6. $y = x^2$

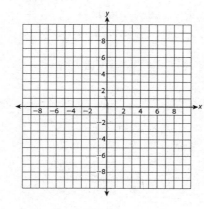

_____

Independent Practice

Use the 4-Step Method for Problem Solving and the strategies you have learned in this lesson to solve the problems in this section.

1   The table below shows a relationship between x and y.

x	y
2	−1
4	3
6	7

Which equation shows the relationship between x and y?

A $y = x - 3$

B $x = y - 3$

C $y = 2x - 5$

D $x = 2y - 5$

hint *The equation must work for all the pairs of values.*

2   Which ordered pair describes a point on the line $y = 4x + 2$?

A $(-1, -2)$

B $(-1, 8)$

C $(0, 6)$

D $(6, 1)$

hint *Test each point in the given equation.*

3   Which answer choice best describes the function below?

$$y = x^2 + 3$$

A horizontal

B vertical

C linear

D non-linear

hint *Create a table with a few coordinate pairs or sketch a graph to test the equation.*

4 Look at the graph below.

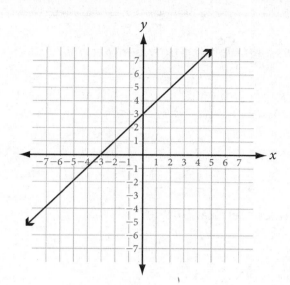

Which function describes this line?

A $f(x) = 2x + 3$
B $f(x) = 2x + 1$
C $f(x) = x + 3$
D $f(x) = x - 3$

hint *Pick two points on the line and test each function.*

5 Which of the following graphs does **not** represent a function?

A

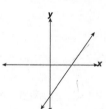

C

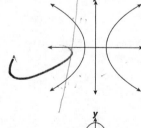

B

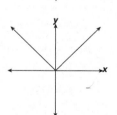

D

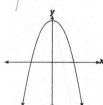

hint *Use the vertical line test to identify the graph that does not represent a function.*

UNIT 3 ● ② ③ ④ ⑤ ⑥

6 The table below shows a relationship between x and y.

x	y
2	8
4	14
6	20
8	26

Which equation describes this relationship?

A $y = 4x$

B $y = 6x + 2$

C $y = x + 6$

D $y = 3x + 2$

hint ▶ *Check more than just the first pair of numbers.*

7 Which set of ordered pairs could represent part of a function?

A (−3, 4), (−2, 2), (−2, 0), (0, 2)

B (1, 4), (2, 4), (3, 4), (4, 4)

C (−5, −1), (−3, 0), (−1, 1), (−1, 3)

D (8, 5), (8, 4), (7, 3), (7, 2)

hint ▶ *Eliminate answer choices that list the same x-value with different y-values.*

8 Complete the table of values for the equation $y = 3x - 4$.

x	y
−2	~0.
−1	
0	
1	
2	

Plot the ordered pairs from the table onto the coordinate grid below. Then, draw a line connecting the points.

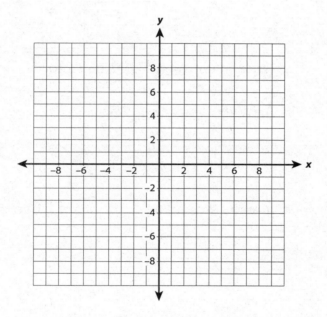

A point on the line has the *y*-coordinate of 8. What is the *x*-coordinate for this point?

Answer_____

hint ▷ *Substitute each x-value into the equation to find the corresponding y-value. Then, plot the points and connect them to draw the line.*

KAP Wrap

Read the question and sample student answer below. Then, use the rubric on page 25 to score the student's work.

---

1 Tracy filled in the table below to show the relationship between *x* and *y*.

x	y
0	15
1	21
2	27
3	33

Write an equation that relates *x* to *y*.

Answer $y = x + 15$

I would give this student a _____ out of 2, because _____

_____

_____

_____

_____

2 Lesson 2
SLOPE-INTERCEPT FORM

Focus Question

How can you use a table or graph to write an equation?

Thinking KAP

The graph below shows the distance Naomi travels.

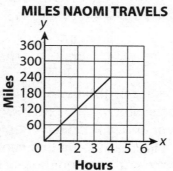

MILES NAOMI TRAVELS

What is the rate that Naomi traveled in **miles per hour**?

_____60_____ miles per hour

If Naomi travels at the same rate, how far will she travel in 6 hours?

_____360_____ miles

Instruction

Rates

A **rate** is a ratio in which the two measurements being compared are in different units. For example, if a 5-pound bag of flour costs $2.50, the rate is $2.50 for 5 pounds. Because this is a ratio, you can set up a proportion to determine the cost of buying other amounts of flour. Fill in the rest of the table to find the cost of each amount of flour.

Cost	$2.50	$5.00	$7.50	$25	$50
Pounds of Flour	5	10	15	50	100

Unit Rates

In a **unit rate**, the second number being compared is always one unit. Unit rates use the term *per* which means "for each." You can find the unit rate by using division or by finding an equivalent fraction. For example, if a car travels 120 miles in 4 hours, the unit rate is:

$$\frac{120 \text{ miles}}{4 \text{ hours}} = \frac{30}{1 \text{ hour}} \text{ or } \underline{} \text{ miles per hour}$$

You can also use graphs to find the unit rate. To find the cost per pound of flour in the table above, plot the amount that comes first in the rate, cost, on the *y*-axis. This is the **dependent variable** because it *depends* on the amount of flour bought. Plot the **independent variable**, pounds, on the *x*-axis.

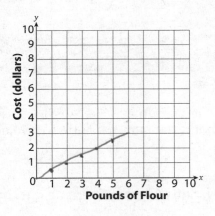

After you graph the points, draw a line. The point (1, *r*) shows the unit rate, *r*.

Use division to check your rate: $\frac{\$2.50}{5} = \underline{0.50}$ per pound.

TRY IT OUT ➡ **Find the unit rate.**

1 A 12-pound bag of potatoes costs $4.80. How much do the potatoes cost per pound?

A $0.40 per pound
B $0.48 per pound
C $0.60 per pound
D $1.20 per pound

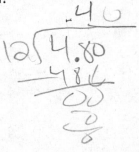

Slope

All linear functions have a constant rate of change called the slope. Slope is the rate of vertical change for each unit of horizontal change. In proportional relationships, like the ones on page 68, the unit rate is the slope and can be found at (1, *r*). Other linear functions, however, do not intersect (0, 0) so you will need other methods to find the slope.

Finding the Slope with Right Triangles

You can use right triangles to find the slope of a line.

- Find two points. Draw a right triangle by moving horizontally and vertically.

- Count the steps you travel in each direction. Use negative numbers to move left or down.

- Divide the vertical distance by the horizontal distance to find the rate.

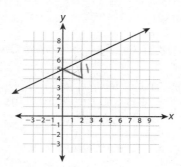

▌TRY IT OUT▐▶ **Find the slope of the line using right triangles.**

Choose two points with integer coordinates and draw the triangle on the graph.

$$\text{Slope} = \frac{\text{vertical change}}{\text{horizontal change}} = \underline{\quad} = \underline{\quad}$$

Check your work. For every 1 unit right do you move $\frac{1}{2}$ unit up? _____

Finding the Slope with Subtraction

The equation below is another way of writing the steps in the triangle method. Think of the two points that you chose as (x_1, y_1) and (x_2, y_2). Now, use subtraction to find the vertical and horizontal changes.

$$\text{slope} = \frac{\text{vertical change}}{\text{horizontal change}} = \frac{y_2 - y_1}{x_2 - x_1}$$

▌TRY IT OUT▐▶ **Find the slope of the line using subtraction.**

Using the graph above, choose two different points. Use the equation to find the slope.

$$\text{slope} = \frac{\text{vertical change}}{\text{horizontal change}} = \frac{y_2 - y_1}{x_2 - x_1} = \underline{\quad\quad} = \underline{\quad}$$

Explain why you get the same slope no matter which pair of points you choose on the line.

You will get same slope because same difference

UNIT 3

The *y*-intercept

Slope-intercept form shows equations in the format $y = mx + b$. The variable *m* represents the slope and *b* represents the *y*-intercept.

The *y*-intercept is the amount that the line has been shifted up or down from the origin. In real-world problems, it often represents a flat fee or starting amount.

ITRY IT OUTI ➡ **Solve the problem below.**

2 Kylie runs a babysitting service. She charges a flat fee of $5, plus $10 per hour. The graph below shows the amount Kylie makes over time.

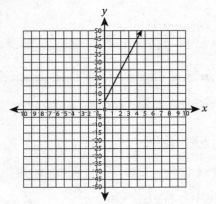

What is the slope of the line?

* Choose two points. _(1, 15) (2, 25)_

* Find the ratio of vertical to horizontal change. _____

What is the *y*-intercept of the line?

* What is the *y*-value where the line crosses the *y*-axis? _5_

  Slope = _10_ **y-intercept =** _5_

Explain what the slope and *y*-intercept represent in this problem.

Flat rate and rate
$10 for 1 hour of
baby sitting

Graphing with Slope and *y*-intercept

Instead of making a table of ordered pairs, you can use the slope and intercept to graph a line.

- First, identify the slope and *y*-intercept using the equation of the line. Pay attention to the signs of the numbers.
- Plot the *y*-intercept.
- Use the slope to find another point on the line.
- Connect the two points to draw the line.

❚TRY IT OUT❚ ➡ **Solve the problem below.**

3 The equation of a line is $y = 2x - 4$. Graph the line on the coordinate plane below.

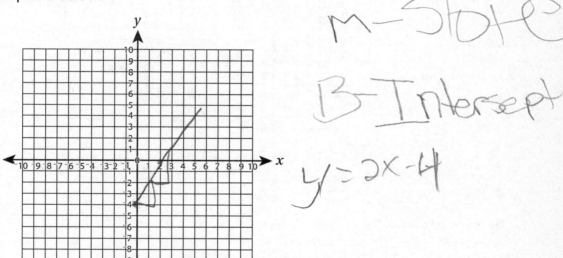

M — slope
B — Intercept
y = 2x - 4

What is the slope, *m*? __2/1__   What is the *y*-intercept, *b*? __−4__

Plot the *y*-intercept on the grid above.

The slope means that for every __1__ unit(s) to the right, the line

moves __2__ unit(s) up / down. (Circle one.)

Use the slope to plot another point on the grid above.

Connect the points to form a line.

Independent Practice

Use the 4-Step Method for Problem Solving and the strategies you have learned in this lesson to solve the problems in this section.

1 What is the slope of this line?

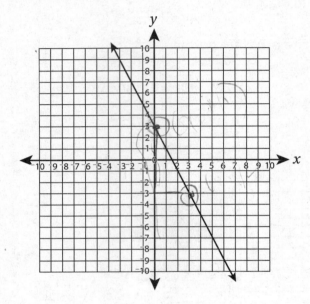

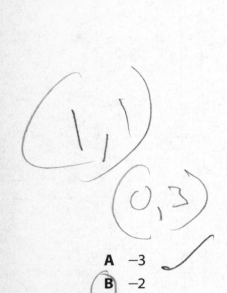

A −3

B −2

C 2

D 3

hint ▷ *Draw a right triangle between two points, then count the length of each side. Divide the vertical change by the horizontal change.*

2 What is the equation of a line with a slope of 4 and a *y*-intercept of −1?

A $y = -x + 4$

B $y = 4x + 1$

C $y = 4x - 1$

D $-y = 4x$

$$y = mx + c$$
$$y = 4x - 1$$

hint ▷ *Substitute the slope for m and the y-intercept for b.*

3   Chelsea did yard work for 7 hours last weekend. Her parents paid her $40. How much did she get paid per hour?

    A $1.75 per hour

    B $5.71 per hour

    C $7.40 per hour

    D $17.50 per hour

hint *Check your answer by multiplying the dollars per hour by the number of hours she worked.*

4   What is the *y*-intercept of this line?

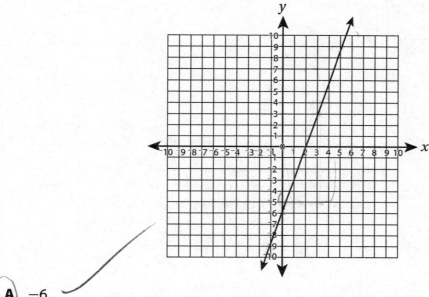

    A −6

    B 2

    C 3

    D 6

hint *What does the y-intercept represent?*

5 A company sells recordable CDs in packages with a different number of CDs in each package. The graph below represents the cost of the different packages.

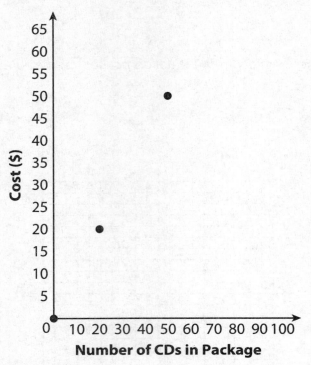

What is the cost of 1 CD?

A $0.50 per CD

B $1 per CD

C $2 per CD

D $20 per CD

hint ▷ *Each point represents the number of CDs in the package and the cost of that package.*

6   The equation of a line is $y = -3x + 1$. Graph the line on the coordinate plane below.

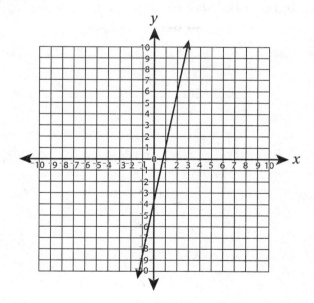

hint ▶ *Plot the y-intercept. Then, use the slope to find another point.*

7   Charlie graphed the line below.

Write the equation for the line.

Answer _____

hint ▶ *Choose two points on the line. Find the vertical over horizontal change to determine the slope.*

KAP Wrap

Read the question and sample student answer below. Then, use the rubric on page 25 to score the student's work.

---

1 The slope of a line is 4 and the *y*-intercept is −2.

What is the equation of the line?

Show your work.

$y = mx + b$

$m = 4$ and $b = 2$

Answer $y = 4x + 2$

I would give this student a _____ out of 2, because _____

_____

_____

_____

Lesson 3
REPRESENTING REAL-WORLD RELATIONSHIPS

Focus Question

How can you translate real-world relationships into equations and graphs?

Thinking KAP

Emily and Jack are counting how many steps it takes to walk across the Brooklyn Bridge.

Emily says that she has walked 10 more steps than Jack has. If Jack has walked *j* steps, what expression could represent the number of steps Emily has taken?

_____

Translating Written Descriptions into Functions

Functions are often written with the variables x and y, but any variables can be used. To translate a written description into an equation, first look for clues.

Clue	Symbol	Example in Words	Example in Symbols
per/for each/ each	$\times$ or $\cdot$	4 books per student *or* Each student had 4 books	$4s$ or $4 \cdot s$
of	$\times$ or $\cdot$	One half of the amount Nina earned	$\frac{1}{2}n$ or $\frac{n}{2}$
entry fee/ base amount/ started with	$+$	The taxi has a starting fee of $3 and then costs $0.25 per mile.	$3 + 0.25m$
discount/took off	$-$	The cost was $10 per hour, with a $15 discount.	$10h - 15$
spent/used	$-$	Beth started with $20 and spent $4 each day.	$20 - 4d$
split equally	$\div$	Three people split their profits equally.	$\frac{p}{3}$
is/was/does/ will be	$=$	If each book is $3, what will the total cost be?	$3b = c$

After you underline the clues, find the independent variable (the input) and dependent variable (the output). Remember that the dependent variable *depends* on the independent variable. Write the dependent variable on one side of the equation. Then, use each clue to find the operations that must be performed on the independent variable to get the dependent variable.

❚TRY IT OUT❚➧   Write an equation to represent the situation.

1   Diane has $50 saved in the bank. She plans to save $20 each week. Write an equation that shows the relationship between the number of weeks, w, and the amount she has saved, s.

What is the dependent variable? _____   Independent variable? _____

Use the clues to find the operations performed on the independent variable and write the equation.

_____

Translating Written Descriptions into Graphs

When you translate a real-world problem to a graph, find which part of the story matches each part of the equation $y = mx + b$.

- The dependent variable is the label for the y-axis.

- The independent variable is the label for the x-axis.

- The rate is the slope. Look for the clues *per* or *each*.

- The starting amount or flat fee is the y-intercept.

▌TRY IT OUT▐➡ **Graph the situation below.**

2 At the beginning of a trip, Mr. Saito has 9 gallons of gas in his car. He uses up 2 gallons of gas during each hour of driving. Graph the relationship between the amount of gas that Mr. Saito has left in his car and the hours he spends driving.

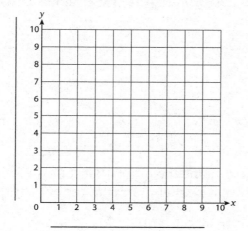

Underline the clues.

What is the independent variable?_____

What is the dependent variable? _____

What is the rate? Should it be positive or negative? _____

What is the starting amount or flat fee?_____

Write the equation and graph it above. _____

After how many hours will Mr. Saito run out of gas? _____ hours
How could you check that your graph is correct?

_____

_____

Shapes of Graphs

Even if no numbers are given, you can use the shape of a graph to tell a story. The most important part is whether the independent variable, on the y-axis, is increasing or decreasing as the dependent variable increases.

Increasing graphs have a positive slope. They go from bottom left to top right.

Decreasing graphs have a negative slope. They go from top left to bottom right.

Proportional graphs intersect the origin, (0, 0). Their starting amount is always 0.

▌TRY IT OUT▐➡ Use the shape of the graphs to answer the questions.

A.

B.

Which graph is increasing? _____ Decreasing? _____

For each story below, name the graph that could be used to show it, or make an X to show that neither graph has the correct shape.

1. Ivor buys some bread. He uses the same number of slices each day to make sandwiches.
   _____

2. At a bowling alley, there is a flat fee to rent a lane. You must pay an additional price for each game.
   _____

3. Each flower costs the same amount. The total cost depends upon the number of flowers.
   _____

Draw the shape of the graph for story 2.

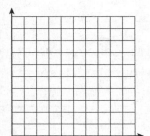

Comparing Linear Functions

Slope is another way of saying *rate of change*. Thus, a higher slope represents a higher rate of change. To compare the rates in two equations, find the slope of each one.

▌TRY IT OUT▌➡ **Use the slope to solve the problems below.**

Chris and Elana joined two different book clubs which ship them new books every month. The number of books Chris receives is shown in the graph. The number of books Elana receives is shown in the equation, where *e* is the total number of books Elana owns and *t* is the time in months.

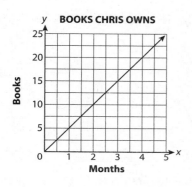

BOOKS ELANA OWNS

$$e = 3t$$

What is the slope of Chris's graph? _____

Who is getting new books at the faster rate?_____

Their friend Vijay is also in a book club. He has already received 10 books. He receives 2 more each month.

Write an equation for the number of books that Vijay receives, *v*, in terms of the time, *t*, in months.

_____

Between Chris, Elana, and Vijay, who is getting new books at the slowest rate?_____

Draw lines to show the number of books that each friend has on Chris's graph.

At 2 months, who has the most books, total?_____

UNIT 3
① ② ● ④ ⑤ ⑥

Independent Practice

Use the 4-Step Method for Problem Solving and the strategies you have learned in this lesson to solve the problems in this section.

1 Ms. Lang is comparing the cost of dried apples at four different stores, A, B, C, and D. Which of the following functions shows the cheapest rate at which she can buy them?

A

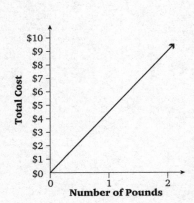

C

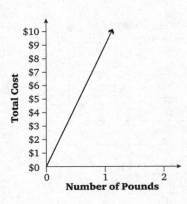

B $c = 3.5p$

D $c = 6p$

> **hint**   *Use the point (1, r) to find the unit rates on the graphs.*

2 Kayla has $600 to spend on her trip. She plans to spend $70 per day. Which equation below shows the relationship between the number of days, *d*, she has been on her trip and the amount of money she has left, *m*?

A $m = 600 - 70d$

B $m = 70d - 600$

C $d = 600 - 70m$

D $d = 70m - 600$

> **hint**   *Which variable is dependent on the other variable?*

KAPLAN KEYS ADVANTAGE
MATHEMATICS GRADE 8

3   Which situation matches the expression $3 + 2x$?

   A   a rate of $5 for every axle on a vehicle

   B   a flat rate of $3, plus an additional $2 for every axle on a vehicle

   C   a flat rate of $2, plus an additional $3 for every axle on a vehicle

   D   a rate of $2 for every axle on a vehicle

hint   *Match each clue in each answer choice to the pieces of the expression.*

4   Of the four linear functions represented below, which has the greatest rate of change?

   A

x	g(x)
−6	13
3	−8
6	−15

   B $2y − 7x = 10$

   C   A number, y, is two more than three times a number, x.

   D

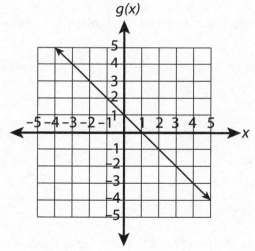

hint   *Write the formula for each answer choice in the form $y = mx + b$.*

UNIT 3

5 Jermaine is raising money for a charity. He earns $12 for each raffle ticket he sells. He also receives a donation of $45. Write an algebraic equation that shows the relationship between *r*, the number of raffle tickets he sells, and *m*, the total amount of money he has earned.

Equation _____

hint ▷ *Which variable depends on the other variable?*

6 A tank full of water has a leak in it. It begins with 10 gallons of water and then loses 1.5 gallons of water each hour.

On the graph below, sketch the **shape** of the line that would show this relationship.

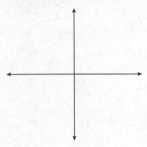

An empty tank has been placed underneath the leaky tank to catch all of the water that drips out.

On the graph below, sketch the **shape** of the line that would show this relationship.

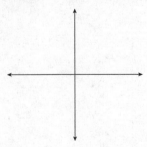

On the lines below, explain how you chose the shape for each graph. Use the terms *increasing* and *decreasing* and indicate whether each slope is positive or negative.

_____

_____

_____

hint ▷ *Can either bucket have a negative amount of water?*

7 A party company is blowing up balloons for an event. The workers have already blown up 50 balloons, and they continue to blow up balloons at a constant rate. Complete the table below to show the number of balloons they have after 3 hours and after 4 hours.

Time in Hours (h)	Number of Balloons (b)
0	
1	
2	
3	
4	

Plot the ordered pairs from the table onto the graph below. Then, draw a line connecting the points.

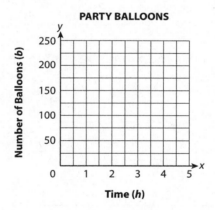

Write an equation to describe the relationship between the number of balloons blown up and the number of hours.

Equation _____

hint ▷ *Find the pattern in the table, then use the pattern to find the missing values.*

8 Moesha is paid $10 for performing at the Poetry Slam. For each person who comes to see her specifically, she is paid an additional $5.

On the graph below, show the relationship between the amount of money Moesha receives, total, and the number of friends she brings. Make sure to:

- Label the axes.
- Draw a line showing the relationship.

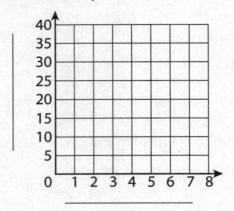

On the lines below, explain how you found the *y*-intercept for your graph.

_____

_____

_____

hint ⟩ *Match each clue to a variable in y = mx + b.*

9 Mica takes her laptop and her phone to a coffee shop to get some work done on the weekend, but she has forgotten her chargers.

Her phone only has 12% of its battery life left and she knows that it loses an additional 3% every 15 minutes. She does not know how quickly her laptop uses up its battery, so she writes down the battery charge several times while she is working.

Minutes Working	Laptop Battery Life Remaining
0	70%
18	61%
30	55%

Write equations that express the amount of battery life left on her phone and laptop as a function of minutes.

Cell Phone _____

Laptop _____

When Mica's phone dies, what percent of her laptop battery life will still be left?

Show your work.

Answer _____ %

hint   *The battery life depends on the amount of time, so battery life is the dependent or y variable.*

UNIT 3
① ② ③ ④ ⑤ ⑥

KAP Wrap

Read the question and sample student answer below. Then, use the rubric on page 25 to score the student's work.

---

1 At a grocery store, customers can buy dry black beans at a rate of $1.10 per pound. If they do not bring their own bags to put the black beans into, they must first purchase a bag for $3.50.

On the graph below, show the relationship between total cost and pounds of beans sold for a customer who does not bring a bag from home.

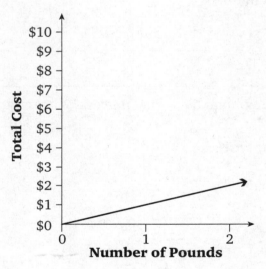

On the lines below, explain the steps you took to draw the graph.

I knew the rate was the slope, so I made the slope 1.1.

I would give this student a _____ out of 2 because_____

_____

_____

_____

4 Lesson 4
SOLVING LINEAR EQUATIONS

Focus Question

What strategies can you use to solve linear equations?

Thinking KAP

Ami is buying supplies for a picnic in the park. Each drink costs $2, and she will also buy a bowl of fruit salad for $10. She has a total of $20 to spend.

If she buys *d* drinks, what equation could she use to find the number of drinks she can buy?

$$2d + 10 = 20$$

Solve the equation to determine how many drinks Ami can buy.

Answer _____5_____ drinks

Solving Equations with Inverse Operations

In an algebraic expression, a number multiplied by a variable is a **coefficient**. Expressions are separated into **terms** by addition or subtraction signs.

coefficient   variable

$2x + 5x - 826$

terms

Solving an equation means finding a value for the variable that makes the equation true. The equation is true when both sides are equal.

When you have a term of 0 (the **additive identity**) or a coefficient of 1 (the **multiplicative identity**), you can remove the term or coefficient from the expression. To use these identities, choose an inverse operation that will result in a term of 0 or a coefficient of 1. Then, apply it to both sides of the equation so that they remain equal.

Remember that each operation must be applied to the entire expression on each side, not just one term.

❚TRY IT OUT❚➡   Use inverse operations to solve the problem below.

1   What is the value of y in the following equation?

$8y + 6 = 78$ $\frac{8y}{8} = \frac{72}{8}$

$8y \quad 72$

$y = 9$

What is the first step to solve this equation?   _add −6_

What is the second step to solve this equation?   _Multiply_

Solve the equation.

One student performed this step first.

$$\frac{8y}{8} + 6 = \frac{78}{8}$$

Explain what is wrong with this student's work.

He skipped the first step
which was to add −6

Equivalent Expressions

Equivalent expressions are expressions that have the same value.

Simplifying with the Order of Operations

When simplifying expressions, remember to use the correct **order of operations**: parentheses, exponents, multiplication and division, then addition and subtraction. You can use the sentence "Please Excuse My Dear Aunt Sally" or the acronym "PEMDAS" to help you remember the correct order. Complete the example below.

$25 - (5 + 3) \div 2 + (7 - 1)^3 = $ _____ $= $ _____

The Distributive Property

The **distributive property** states that multiplying a number by a sum has the same value as multiplying the number by each part of the sum. This is called **expanding**.

$$3(y - 4) = 3y - 12 \qquad\qquad \frac{1}{4}(20x + 8) = 5x + 2$$

Factoring

You can also use the distributive property to find the common factor of the terms in a sum. Factoring is the opposite of the steps above. For example, in $12x + 9$, both terms are divisible by 3, so it has the same value as $3(4x + 3)$.

Combining Like Terms

If terms have the same variable, you can combine the coefficients through addition or subtraction. Remember that you can only combine *like* terms—terms with the same variables or without any variables. Complete the example below.

$(5a - 6) - (2a + 9) = 5a - 6 - 2a$ _____ $= 5a - 2a$ _____ $= 3a$ _____

▌TRY IT OUT▐ ➡ Find the equivalent expressions.

Use the distributive property to expand.

1. $5(2g + 5) = $ 10g + 25

2. $-8(3a - 4) = $ -24a + 32

Factor out.

3. $20h - 16 = $ 4(5h -4)

4. $-21m + 35 = $ 7(3m+5)

Simplify.

5. $(2g + 9) - (g + 2) = $ g+7

6. $(1 - 6s) + (11 + 2s) = $ 12-4s

Use the order of operations to simplify.

7. $13f + 2(f + 4) = $

13f + ~~2(f+4)~~

2f + 8

15 f+8

8. $\frac{10d + 4}{2} + d = $ 6d+2

Handwritten margin work:

336
×6
‾‾‾
216

$25 - (5 + 3) \div 2 + (7 - 1)^3$
  8   6

$25 - 8 \div 2 + 216$

© 2013 Kaplan, Inc.

Backsolving

When questions have variables in the problem and numbers in the answer choices, you can Backsolve.

Backsolving
• Substitute each answer choice into the problem.
• Eliminate answer choices that do not make the equation true.

❙TRY IT OUT❙▶ **Use Backsolving to solve the problem below.**

2 What value of x makes the equation $4x - 8 = 28$ true?

    A 5   (**C**) 9

    B 7   **D** 16

(handwritten: $+8$ $+8$ / $4x = 36$ / $\div 4$ $\div 4$ / $x = 9$)

If an answer does not make the equation true, eliminate it.

Picking Numbers

When questions have variables in the answer choices, you can Pick Numbers.

Picking Numbers
• Pick a number for the variable or unknown.
• Compute the answer with your number.
• Compute each answer choice and look for the same value.

❙TRY IT OUT❙▶ **Use Picking Numbers to solve the problem below.**

3 Marina played tennis for 4 hours less than twice the number of hours, h, Chantal played. Which expression could be used to find the number of hours Marina played tennis?

    A $4h - 2$ (**C**) $2h - 4$

    B $4 - 2h$ **D** $2 - 4h$

• Pick a number for the number of hours Chantal played tennis. Try $h = 3$.

• Find the number of hours Marina played tennis, if Chantal played for 3 hours: $2 \times 3 = 6$. Four hours less than that is $6 - 4$, or 2.

• Substitute 3 into each answer choice to find one equal to 2.

Equations with Infinite Solutions or No Solutions

Most equations that we have looked at so far have one solution. For example, in the equation $3x = -9$, the equation is true for $x = -3$, but not for any other number like $x = 2$.

$$3x = -9 \qquad\qquad 3(-3) = -9 \qquad\qquad 3(2) \neq 9$$

Look at the equations below. Try several different values for the variables in each one. What happens?

$$3y = 2y + y \qquad\qquad\qquad 3z + 4 = 3z + 2$$

infinite solution _no solution_

You can identify an equation with **infinite solutions** when both sides have been simplified until the variables are removed, leaving two numbers that are equal to each other.

You can identify an equation with **no solution** when both sides have been simplified until the variables are removed, leaving two numbers that are not equal to each other.

Simplify each equation above.

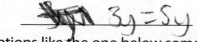 $3y = 5y$ _____ $4 = 2$

Equations like the one below sometimes confuse students. Try to simplify it. Does it have one solution, infinite solutions, or no solutions?

$$5a = 2a + a \qquad$$ _NO solution_

You might think that the equation above has no solutions if you get the intermediate step $2a = 0$. However, dividing both sides by 2 shows that this equation is true for $a = 0$.

∎TRY IT OUT∎ **Find the solution for each equation, or write "no solution" or "infinite solutions."**

1. $6g + 4 - 2g = 3 + 4g - 5$ _____ NO

2. $3m - 2 + m = 7 + 5m + 1$ _____ No solution

3. $13 + 2j - 5 = 9j + 8 - 7j$ _____ infinite solution

4. $4c - 7 + 5 = -2 + 2c$ _____

Independent Practice

Use the 4-Step Method for Problem Solving and the strategies you have learned in this lesson to solve the problems in this section.

1 Find the value of *x* in the equation below.

$$-4x - 7 = 25$$

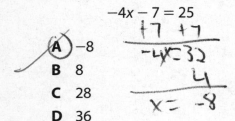

A −8
B 8
C 28
D 36

hint *Keep track of the negative sign as you isolate the variable.*

2 Paulo wants to solve the equation $7x - 5 = 23$. Which steps could Paulo follow to find the solution?

A Divide both sides by 7. Then, add 5 to both sides.
B Subtract 5 from both sides. Then, divide both sides by 7.
C Multiply both sides by 7. Then, subtract 5 from both sides.
D Add 5 to both sides. Then, divide both sides by 7.

hint *Solve the equation using inverse operations. Then, choose the answer choice that matches the steps you took.*

3 Julio and Roberto get paid by their parents to do chores. The amount of money that Julio, *j*, and Roberto, *r*, made in dollars can be represented by the equation below.

$$3j + 2.75 = r$$

If Roberto made $15.50, how much did Julio make?

A $2.42
B $4.25
C $6.08
D $38.25

hint *First, substitute in the value for r. Then, solve for j. You can also use Backsolving.*

4 Which expression is equivalent to the expression below?

$$8x + 12$$

A $2(4x + 2)$

B $4(2x + 3)$

C $8(x + 4)$

Ⓓ $12(x + 1)$

hint   *Try the distributive property on each answer choice. Use Picking Numbers to check your answer.*

5 Evaluate the equation below for *r*.

$$3r - 5 + 2r = -9 + 5r + 7$$

A $r = 0$

B $r = -2$

Ⓒ no solution

D infinite solutions

hint   *Simplify until you have either r equal to a number or two numbers without a variable.*

6 Evaluate the equation below to find the value of *x* that makes it true.

$$\frac{2}{5}x - 5 = 13$$

A 6.4

Ⓑ 14.4

C 20

D 45

hint   *Remember that the multiplicative inverse of a fraction is its reciprocal. What can you multiply $\frac{2}{5}$ by to get a coefficient of 1?*

UNIT 3 ① ② ③ ④ ⑤ ⑥

7 Evaluate the expression below for *t*.

$$-6 + 7t + 2 = -4t + 8 + 11t$$

Answer _____

On the lines below, explain how you know that your answer is correct.

_____

_____

_____

hint *Simplify the equation. Explain how the simplified statement proves your answer.*

8 Charis is trying to write an equation that has infinite solutions. She wants her equation to use the variable *c* and have at least two terms on each side.

Write an equation that Charis could use.

Equation _____

On the lines below, explain how you chose the terms to place on each side of the equation.

_____

_____

_____

_____

hint *Start with an equation that has just one term on each side that you know will work. Then, add another term to each side.*

9 Factor to find an equivalent expression.

$$49k + 14$$

Expression _____

On the lines below, explain how you know that the expressions are equivalent.

_____

_____

_____

hint Find the GCF. Then, write the expression as a product of the GCF and a sum.

10 Simplify the expression below.

$$\frac{5}{6}(36y - 24) - 3(y + 7)$$

Show your work.

Expression _____

hint Use PEMDAS. Multiplying by a fraction is the same as multiplying by its numerator and dividing by its denominator.

UNIT 3
① ② ③ ④ ⑤ ⑥

KAP Wrap

Read the question and sample student answer below. Then, use the rubric on page 25 to score the student's work.

---

1 Abby's teacher wrote the following equation on the board.

$$4x - 10 = 42$$

Solve the equation for *x*.

Show your work.

$x = 8$

Answer _____8_____

I would give this student a _____ out of 2, because _____

_____

_____

_____

5

Lesson 5
SOLVING SIMULTANEOUS LINEAR EQUATIONS

Focus Question

How can you use simultaneous equations to solve problems?

Thinking KAP

Paula is exploring two different linear equations. Help her to fill in the tables below with values for x and y that make each equation true.

$y = x + 3$	
x	y
0	3
1	4
2	5
3	6

$y = 2x$	
x	y
0	0
1	2
2	4
3	6

Paula notices something interesting about the value $x = 3$. Describe what she notices about the y-coordinates when $x = 3$ in each equation.

If you subtract 3 from that you get Y.

If Paula graphed the lines for these two equations, what would happen at the point (3, 6)?

Graphing Systems of Equations

When you have one variable and one equation, the solution is a number that can be substituted for the variable to make the equation true. For example, $4x = 8$ when $x = 2$.

When you have two variables in one equation, many ordered pairs, (x, y) can make the equation true. For example, $y = 4x$ for the points $(0, 0)$, $(1, 4)$, $(2, 8)$ and so on.

A **system of equations** is a set of equations that share the same variables. The solution to the system is the set of numbers that make all the equations true **simultaneously**. In a graph, the point where the lines intersect gives the values for x and y that make the equations true at the same time.

❚ TRY IT OUT ❚ ➡ **Solve the problem below by graphing.**

1 Graph the equations below.

$$\begin{cases} y = 2x - 4 \\ y = -x + 5 \end{cases}$$

What point represents the solution to this system of equations?

• Graph the first line using the slope and y-intercept.

slope = _____ y-intercept = _____

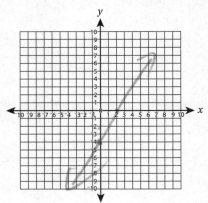

• Graph the second line using the slope and y-intercept.

slope = _____ y-intercept = _____

• What point shows the solution to the system of equations? _____

© 2013 Kaplan, Inc.

Checking Your Work

When graphing systems of equations, you can check your work by testing the solution in both equations.

- Substitute the values for x and y into the first equation and simplify. If the result is a true statement, the point is correct for the first equation.

- Substitute the values for x and y into the second equation and simplify. If the result is a true statement, the point is the solution of the system.

▌TRY IT OUT▐➡ Check your work by testing the solution.

Test your solution to the system of equations on the previous page.

My solution is _____.

Test the solution in the first equation.

$$y = 2x - 4$$

Does the solution make the first equation true? _____

Test the solution in the second equation.

$$y = -x + 5$$

Does the solution make the second equation true? _____

Solving Systems of Equations Algebraically

You can also solve systems of equations with algebra.

- Isolate one variable in the first equation.
- Substitute the equivalent expression for that variable into the other equation.
- Solve for the second variable.
- Substitute in the value of the second variable to find the first variable.

I TRY IT OUT I ➡ **Solve the system of equations algebraically.**

$$-x + y = 1 \qquad 2x + y = -2$$

Isolate y in the first equation: _____

Substitute the expression into the second equation for y:

$$2x + \underline{\hspace{2cm}} = -2$$

Solve for x.

$$x = \underline{\hspace{1.5cm}}$$

Substitute the value you found for x into the first equation above. Then, solve for y.

$$-x + y = 1$$

$$-\underline{\hspace{2cm}} + y = 1$$

$$y = \underline{\quad 0 \quad}$$

Check your solution by substituting it in each of the original equations.

$$-(-1) + 0 = 1 \checkmark$$
$$1 + 0 = 1 \checkmark$$

A system of linear equations can have exactly one solution, infinitely many solutions (if the lines are the same), or no solution (if the lines are parallel and do not intersect).

I TRY IT OUT I ➡ **Determine how many solutions each system has.**

1. $\begin{cases} 2x + y = 7 \\ 2x + y = 8 \end{cases}$ 2. $\begin{cases} -2x + y = 3 \\ -4x + 2y = 6 \end{cases}$

     No solution   infinite solution

Solving Problems Using Systems of Equations

You can solve problems by writing and solving systems of equations.

▮ TRY IT OUT ▮ ➡ **Write and solve a system of equations to solve the problem.**

A salad bar sells two sizes of pre-made salads. A regular salad sells for $5. A small salad is $3. On Monday, the salad bar sold 80 pre-made salads and made $280. How many of each size of salad did they sell?

Write a system of equations to represent what is happening in the problem. Let *r* equal the number of regular salads sold, and let *s* equal the number of small salads sold.

Write an equation to represent the total number of pre-made salads sold.

$s + r = 80$

Write another equation to represent the amount of money earned from selling each type of salad.

$5r \quad 3s = 80$

Solve the system of equations algebraically.

$r + s = 80$

Regular Salads _____   Small Salads _____

Check your solution by substituting it in each of the original equations.

Does your answer make sense? _____

Independent Practice

Use the 4-Step Method for Problem Solving and the strategies you have learned in this lesson to solve the problems in this section.

1 Which system of equations will have exactly one point of intersection?

A $\begin{cases} y = 2x + 13 \\ y = 2x - 3 \end{cases}$

B $\begin{cases} y = -x - 10 \\ y = x + 27 \end{cases}$

C $\begin{cases} y = \frac{3}{4}x + 15 \\ y = 0.75x + 15 \end{cases}$

D $\begin{cases} y = -x + 12 \\ y = -x + 24 \end{cases}$

hint *Parallel lines have the same slope and do not intersect.*

2 Which ordered pair is a solution to this system of equations?

$\begin{cases} y = 3x \\ x + y = -32 \end{cases}$

A (−24, −8)

B (−8, −24)

C (8, 24)

D (24, 8)

hint *You can Backsolve. Substitute each answer choice into the original equations.*

3 Which statement is true about systems of equations with an infinite number of solutions?

A The equations must have different slopes.

B Both equations must have different *y*-intercepts.

C Both equations can be represented by the same line.

D Both equations can be represented by parallel lines.

hint ▷ *A solution is a set of points (x, y) that makes both equations true.*

4 How many solutions does this system of equations have?

$$\begin{cases} 12y + 10x = 16 \\ 5x + 6y = 8 \end{cases}$$

A exactly one solution

B exactly two solutions

C no solutions

D infinite solutions

hint ▷ *Make the equations look as similar as possible, then compare any traits that are different.*

5 A system of equations is shown below.

$$\begin{cases} y = 2x + 7 \\ y = 4x - 9 \end{cases}$$

Solve the system of equations.

Show your work.

y = _____   *x* = _____

On the lines below, explain why this pair of values solves this system of equations.

_____

_____

hint ▷ *Use substitution to create an equation with only one variable in it.*

6 At a basketball game, adult tickets cost $22 and children's tickets cost $15. A group spent $228 to purchase 11 tickets.

On the lines below, write the equations that can be used to represent the problem.

Equations $A + C = 11$ $22A + 15C = 228$

Find the number of adults and children who went to the game.

Show your work.

Number of adults 9 **Number of children** 2

> **hint** Write an equation for the number of people who went and another equation for the prices they paid for the tickets.

7 Jamie wants to call his friend in Argentina. He is trying to choose between two phone cards. MightyCalls charges 6.2 cents per minute. LuckyCalls charges 50 cents per connection and then 4.1 cents per minute. Both cards round up to the nearest whole minute when charging for calls.

Write equations that express the cost of each plan as a function of minutes used.

MightyCalls _____ **LuckyCalls** _____

Jamie thinks that he will only talk to his friend for 20 minutes. Which card would be best if this were the only call that he made?

Answer _____

Jamie's brother wants to talk to the friend in the same call. Based upon the rates for the two cards, give Jamie advice on which card would be a better option, depending on the total amount of time they will spend on the call.

_____

_____

> **hint** The solution to the system of equations is the point where their values are the same.

8   Kittson wants to solve this system of equations by graphing.

$$\begin{cases} y = -x + 5 \\ y = 5x - 1 \end{cases}$$

Graph both equations on the coordinate plane below.

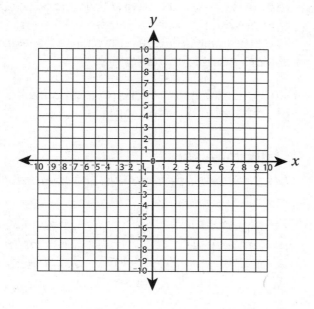

What point represents the solution to this system of equations?

Answer   1 and 4

Check your solution by substituting it in each of the original equations.

Show your work.

hint   *Graph each equation using the slope and y-intercept, and then find each point of intersection.*

KAP Wrap

Read the question and sample student answer below. Then, use the rubric on page 24 to score the student's work.

---

1 Joshua is choosing between two high-speed internet providers. One provider charges a $40 set-up fee and costs $30 per month. The other provider does not charge a set-up fee, but charges $50 per month for the service.

Find the month in which the total price he pays for either provider would be the same.

Show your work.

Let c = cost of each plan. Let m equal the number of months.

First provider: *Second provider:*

$c = 30m + 40$ $c = 50m$

$50m = 30m + 40$ $c = 50 \cdot 2$

$20m = 40$ $c = 100$

$m = 2$

Answer _____2_____ months

On the lines below, explain which service is a better deal if he wants to keep the service for 3 months.

The first provider would cost 30(3) + 40 = $130. The second provider would cost 50(3) = $150. So the first provider is a better deal.

I would give this student a _____ out of 3 because _____

_____

_____

_____

6 Lesson 6
MULTI-STEP PROBLEMS WITH LINEAR EQUATIONS

Focus Question
How can you use linear equations to solve problems with ratios and geometry?

Thinking KAP

Mateo has just placed a fence around his patio, as shown below. (There is no fence on the side that touches his house.)

Each square in his patio is *x* feet long and *x* feet wide. Write an equation that you can use to find the length of the whole fence, in terms of *x*.

_____

Instruction

Solving Relationship Questions with Variables

Some algebra questions will require you to remember basic geometry formulas.

Rectangle Perimeter: _____

Rectangle Area: _____   **Triangle Area:** _____

First, write the equation that you need. Then, use substitution to fill in the information that you know and solve.

▎**TRY IT OUT**▎➡ Use geometry equations to solve.

1 A triangle has an area of 120. Its dimensions are shown below. What is the value of *n*?

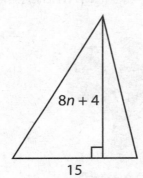

8n + 4

15

Show your work.

*Answer*_____

2 A rectangle's length is 3 inches longer than half its width. If its perimeter is 21 inches, what is its width?

Draw a picture. Label each dimension.

*Answer*_____ inches

Solving Ratio Questions with Variables

Some questions that could be solved with equations don't tell you that you can use variables, so you need to add your own.

Ratio questions that can be solved with tape diagrams can also be solved with equations. If there are 4 apples for every 5 oranges, you can multiply 4 and 5 by any number and keep the same ratio. This is like saying that the number of apples is $4x$ and the number of oranges is $5x$.

❚TRY IT OUT❚ ➡ **Use variables to solve the problems with equations.**

3 The ratio of land snakes to tree snakes in a zoo is 4:3. If there are 259 snakes in the zoo, how many are tree snakes?

Write an equation for the number of snakes, then solve.

*Answer*_____ tree snakes

4 A rectangular parking lot has sides in a ratio of 2:3. The perimeter of the parking lot is 250 meters. Determine the dimensions, in meters, of the parking lot.

Draw a picture of the parking lot. Use variables to describe the length of each side.

Write an equation for the perimeter.

Solve for the variable.

Use the value of the variable to find the length of each side.

*Answer*_____ meters wide and _____ meters long

Two Points Determine a Line

If two points are drawn on a coordinate grid, this is all the information you need to determine the line that intersects them. If you don't have a grid, you can still use the coordinates to find the equation for the line.

First, use the change in y divided by the change in x to find the slope.

For the points (3, −8) and (2, −6), the slope is _____

Substitute the slope into $y = mx + b$ form: _____

Substitute in one point to solve for b. Try (3, −8):

Write the equation with b: _____

Use the other point to check. _____

If the two points are in a story problem, start by writing them as coordinates.

▌TRY IT OUT▐➡ **Use the steps above to solve the problem.**

5   A bus tour company charges a flat fee for renting out the bus, and an additional amount for each person. If the price is quoted at $382 for 12 people and $430 for 16 people, what equation can be used to find the cost for any number of people?

What is the cost per person?

Answer $ _____ per person

What is the flat fee?

Answer $_____

What equation can be used to find the cost for any number of people?

Equation _____

Ratios and Equations in Geometry

Some questions about ratios or equations may look like geometry problems. Remember to use the 4-Step Method and look for clues that you can use to write a ratio or equation. When two shapes are similar, this means that you can write a ratio between the sides of one and the sides of the other.

▌TRY IT OUT▐ ➡ **Look for clues and make a plan to solve each part.**

6 In the diagram below, △*PST* is similar to △*PQR*.

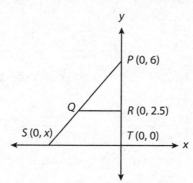

Part A: What is the scale factor from △*PST* to △*PQR*?
What clues do you have?

_____

Write a ratio between the side lengths that you know: _____

Answer_____

Part B: If the slope of PS is $\frac{5}{4}$, what is the value of *x* for coordinate *S*?

What clues do you have? _____

Write an equation for the line. _____

Solve the equation when *y* = 0. _____

Answer_____

Part C: Using the information from parts (A) and (B), what is the length of *QR*?
What clues do you have?

_____

Use a proportion: _____

Answer_____

UNIT 3
①②③④⑤

Independent Practice

1 Mr. Wilson wants to remodel his house. The cost of getting new carpet installed is a linear function with respect to the area of the floor in square feet. For the type of carpet he has chosen, installing 150 square feet of carpeting costs $670 and installing 525 square feet costs $2,170.

Write a linear function as an equation to model the relationship between the cost of installing carpet and the square feet of carpet installed.

Equation _____

On the line below, explain the meaning of the slope in the context of the problem.

_____

On the lines below, explain one possible meaning for the *y*-intercept in the context of the problem.

_____

_____

> **hint** *Think of the number of square feet and the corresponding cost as a coordinate pair.*

2 The length of a rectangular projector screen is 8 cm more than its width. If the length is increased by 7 cm and width is decreased by 4 cm, the perimeter of the board is 102 cm.

Determine the dimensions, in cm, of the projector board.

Show your work.

Answer _____ cm wide and _____ cm long

> **hint** *Draw a picture. Choose only one variable, w or l, and use it to describe the other side.*

3 A taxi cab company charges the same amount for each mile driven, plus a flat-fee for each trip. The receipts for two trips are shown below.

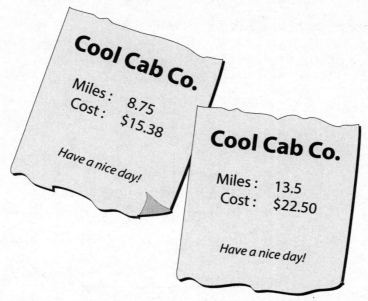

What is the cost of each mile that is driven, **not** counting the flat-fee?

Answer $ _____

What is the flat-fee?

Answer $ _____

On the lines below, explain how you found your answers.

_____

_____

_____

_____

hint ▶ *The number of miles is the independent variable, x. So the first point is (8.75, 13.5).*

4 In the coordinate plane below, △*PQR* is similar to △*PST*.

What is the value of *x*?

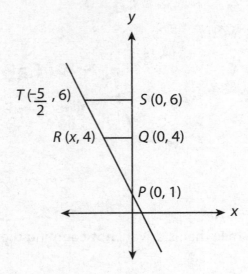

Show your work.

Answer_____

hint ▷ *Label every length you know on the diagram.*

5 Kendra has to create an isosceles triangle using the side relationships shown below, such that the perimeter is 20 inches.

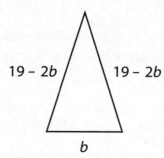

$19 - 2b$ $\qquad$ $19 - 2b$

b

What is the length of the base of the isosceles triangle?

Show your work.

Answer_____

hint ▸ *Write an equation, then combine like terms.*

UNIT 3 ① ② ③ ④ ⑤

KAP Wrap

Read the question and sample student answer below. Then, use the rubric on page 25 to score the student's work.

---

1 Write an equation for the linear function shown in the table below.

x	−3	3	9
f(x)	11	3	−5

Show your work.

I will use the points (−3, 11) and (3, 3).

Slope: $\dfrac{11-3}{-3-3} = \dfrac{8}{-6} = -\dfrac{4}{3}$

Solve for b: $f(x) = -\dfrac{4}{3}x + b$

$3 = -\dfrac{4}{3}(3) + b$

$3 = -4 + b$

$7 = b$

Equation $\underline{\quad f(x) = -\dfrac{4}{3}x + 7 \quad\quad\quad\quad\quad}$

I would give this student a _____ out of 2 because _____

_____

_____

_____

UNIT 4 Strategies for Statistics and Probability

1 Lesson 1
SCATTER PLOTS

Focus Question

How can you use scatter plots to show relationships between related data sets?

Thinking KAP

The students in Ms. Cho's class each measured their height and arm span. They showed their results on the scatter plot below.

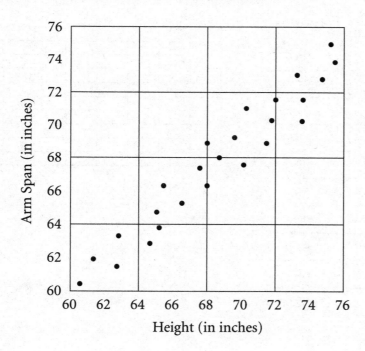

What relationship is shown in the scatter plot?

_____

_____

If you drew a best-fit line to represent the data, what would be the approximate slope of the line? _____

Instruction

Scatter Plots

Scatter plots are used to determine whether a relationship exists between two sets of measurements taken from the same members of a population. When two variables are measured, the data is called **bivariate** and can be written as an ordered pair.

TRY IT OUT ➡ **Use the data to create a scatter plot and answer the questions.**

1 The table below shows the number of hours that 10 students spent studying and the grades they received on the test.

Create a scatter plot on the line below.

Hours Studied	Grade
8	98
6	95
3	77
7	100
6	92
2	65
4	80
5	92
1	60
4	82

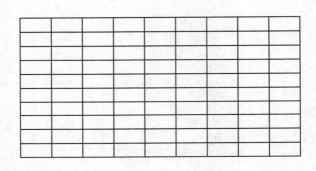

Which variable is the dependent variable? _____

Label the axes, choose a scale for each axis, and graph the data. Do not connect the points.

Describe the relationship between hours spent studying and test grades.

_____

_____

Relationships in Scatter Plots

Linear Relationships

Scatter plots show how two variables are related to each other. When the data makes a line or curve, there is a **correlation** between the variables.

- A **positive correlation** shows that the *y*-variable *increases* as the *x*-variable increases. A line drawn through these points would have a positive slope.

- A **negative correlation** shows that the *y*-variable *decreases* as the *x*-variable increases. A line drawn through these points would have a negative slope.

- A **curvilinear** or **non-linear relationship** follows a curve.

- When the data does not form a shape like a line, it has **no correlation**.

Identify the correlations in each of the scatter plots below.

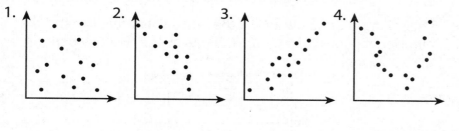

_____ _____ _____ _____

When the points are very close to forming a line, there is a **strong correlation**. When the points are more spread out but still show a trend, there is a **weak correlation**.

Which graph above has the strongest correlation? _____

▌TRY IT OUT▐➡   **Solve the problem below.**

2   Carlos is plotting a data set on the scatter plot below. What kind of correlation does the plot show?

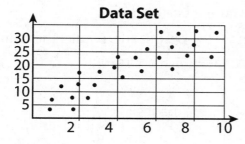

A   strong positive

B   weak positive

C   weak negative

D   no correlation

Best-Fit Lines

When there is a linear correlation in data, you can approximate it with a **line of best fit**. In a strong positive or a strong negative correlation, the data points are very close to the line of best fit.

To draw a best-fit line, hold your ruler near where you think the line should be, or lightly draw your first guess. Then, make sure that there are about the same number of points above and below the ruler, and that the points above and below are about the same distance from the line. Draw when you find the line that is closest to the middle.

▌TRY IT OUT▐ ➡ **Use a best-fit line to answer the questions below.**

3 The scatter plot below shows the hours spent reading and the number of pages read by 18 students over a two-day period.

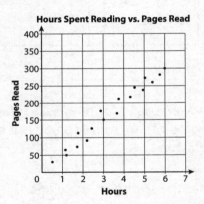

Think about the data. Should your line of best fit pass through the origin?
_____

Use your ruler to draw a best-fit line to approximate the data.

Pick two points and use them to find the slope. _____

Write the equation for the best-fit line. _____

Using the equation for the best-fit line, predict the number of pages that a typical student can read in $3\frac{1}{4}$ hours.

Answer _____ pages

Extrapolation, Interpolation, and Descriptions

You can use best-fit lines to make predictions. Data with a strong correlation to the best-fit line will provide a more accurate prediction than data with a weak correlation.

Interpolation is a prediction that is within the range of the data set. On page 124, you interpolated the number of pages read within 3.25 hours, because 3.25 is between 0.5 and 6. **Extrapolation** assumes that the same relationship that happens within the data continues beyond the range of the data.

▌TRY IT OUT▌➧ **Use extrapolation to solve the problem below.**

4 The scatter plot below shows the number of flowers on a sample of magnolia trees based on the age of the tree.

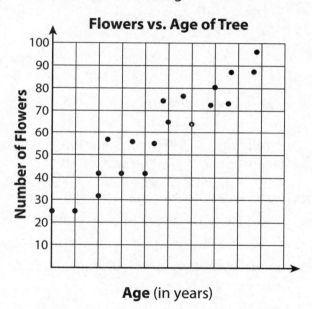

How many flowers would you expect on a tree that was 15 years old?

Draw a best-fit line.

Use two points to find the equation for the best-fit line. _____

Substitute in the value 15 years.

How many flowers would you expect on a 15-year-old tree? _____

Descriptions

Recall from Unit 3 that a slope is a rate that can be used to describe how quickly a value increases or decreases. The y-intercept or smallest x-value may provide a starting point. For example, you can describe the graph above with this statement:

Magnolia trees produce about 25 flowers their first year. After that, they produce about 7.5 additional flowers each year.

Independent Practice

Use the 4-Step Method for Problem Solving and the strategies you have learned in this lesson to solve the problems in this section.

Use the information below to answer questions 1 and 2.

The scatter plot below shows the average temperature and the number of visitors to the beach for each day during the month of May.

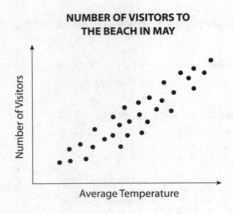

NUMBER OF VISITORS TO THE BEACH IN MAY

Number of Visitors

Average Temperature

1 Which statement best describes the relationship between the average daily temperature and the number of visitors to the beach, as shown on the scatter plot?

A The number of beach visitors increases as the average temperature increases.

B The number of beach visitors decreases as the average temperature increases.

C The number of beach visitors increases as the average temperature decreases.

D There is no relationship between the number of beach visitors and the average temperature.

hint *Read the axes carefully to determine what they mean.*

2 Which statement describes the correlation between the number of visitors and the average temperature?

A negative

B non-linear

C positive

D no correlation

hint *The sign on the correlation matches the sign of the slope in the best-fit line.*

3 Which of the following equations is closest to the best-fit line for the graph below?

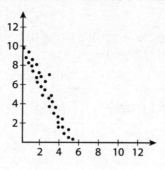

A $y = -2x + 10$

B $y = -\frac{1}{2}x + 10$

C $y = \frac{1}{2}x + 10$

D $y = 2x + 10$

hint *Is the slope positive or negative?*

4 The population growth of Farmington is shown on the scatter plot below.

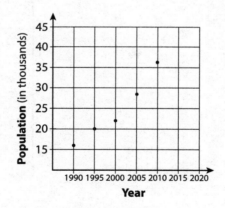

If the same pattern of population growth continues linearly, what will the population of Farmington be in the year 2020?

A 38,000

B 44,000

C 49,000

D 52,000

hint *Draw a best-fit line. You can use the graph to find the value of the line at 2020 without finding the equation.*

5   Celeste is curious about her sister Anouk's growth over time. The table below shows Anouk's weight, in pounds, at each year of age.

Age (years)	Weight (pounds)
1	17
2	23
3	25
4	33
5	40
6	48
7	54

Using the data, construct a scatter plot to show the relationship between Anouk's age and weight.

Be sure to:
- title the graph
- label each axis
- give each axis a scale
- plot all points

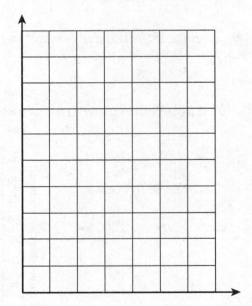

Find the equation for the line of best fit.

_____

Would this equation be useful for extrapolating Anouk's weight at age 20? Why or why not?

_____

_____

_____

hint   *Do people's weights change by the same amount throughout their lives?*

6   Mr. Cooper keeps track of the book sales made at his store. For each order, he plots the number of books in the order and the total cost of the order, as shown in the scatter plot below.

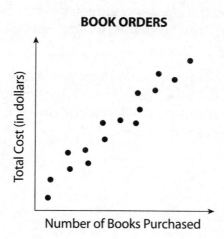

BOOK ORDERS

Total Cost (in dollars)

Number of Books Purchased

Mr. Cooper is trying to draw a best-fit line, but is not sure whether it should go through the origin.

On the lines below, explain to him why his best-fit line should or should not go through the origin.

_____

_____

On the lines below, give a written description of the information that Mr. Cooper can conclude from his best-fit line. Be sure to include the starting point and the meaning of the rate.

_____

_____

_____

hint   *What does the value x = 0 mean? What does the value y = 0 mean?*

KAP Wrap

Read the question and sample student answer below. Then, use the rubric on page 25 to score the student's work.

---

1 Frank is a party planner. He uses a scatter plot, shown below, with the costs and number of guests from 15 parties he has planned to help his customers predict the amount they should expect to spend.

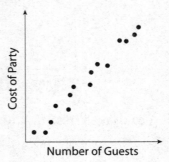

On the lines below, describe the correlation between the cost of a party and the number of guests.

There is a strong positive correlation.

A competitor, Kelia, promises that she can host parties at a lower cost per guest than Frank can. If she made a scatter plot, how would her best-fit line be different from Frank's?

On the lines below, explain how the slope of Kelia's best-fit line would be different from Frank's.

Kelia's best-fit line would have a higher slope because her parties cost less money for the same number of guests. Both of their best-fit lines should intersect the origin, because a party with 0 guests costs $0.

I would give this student a _____ out of 2 because _____

_____

_____

_____

_____

2 Lesson 2
ANALYZING BIVARIATE RELATIONSHIPS

Focus Question
What conclusions can you draw from bivariate data?

Thinking KAP

Julissa takes the bus to school in the mornings. She made a scatter plot to show the number of miles the buses travel and the time they take to travel those distances.

Describe the relationship between the time in minutes and the distance traveled by the bus.

_____

_____

_____

_____

_____

Instruction

Clusters and Outliers

Interpreting data in a scatter plot requires critical thinking. In addition to linear or non-linear relationships, it is important to notice how close or far away points are from each other.

Clusters are areas on a graph where many data points are close together. They represent more common pairs of data points, which may be important in identifying trends. Clusters may or may not be part of linear relationships.

An **outlier** is a point that does not fit into the pattern created by the other points. Sometimes outliers are caused by mistakes in how the data is collected. For example, if everyone in the class reported their height in inches but one student reported her height in centimeters, you could analyze that data point to discover the error.

Other outliers may tell you something important about the data. For example, in a study, 100 people might take a medication to lower cholesterol. If cholesterol levels decrease in 95 people but increase in 5 people, understanding the effects on those 5 people could help the researchers improve the medicine or determine which patients it could help the most.

▌TRY IT OUT▐▶ **Look for clusters and outliers to answer the questions.**

In the graphs below, circle the clusters and put squares around the outliers.

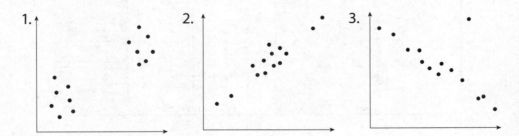

Match each graph to the data set that was used to create it.

Students compare their height and weight. Most students are near the middle in both categories. _____

Most students who spent more hours exercising also spent less time watching TV. One student exercises several hours each day while watching TV. _____

The length and weight of the fish in a pond are compared. There are only large koi fish and small feeder fish, but no medium-sized fish. _____

Causation versus Correlation

Causation indicates that one variable in a study *causes* the other. For example, the first graph supports the conclusion that spending more time reading *causes* people to read more pages.

However, not every trend indicates causation. For example, in the second graph there is a strong negative **correlation**. But does purchasing more soup *cause* people to buy less milk? Or are both of these trends caused by some other factor like the temperature outside?

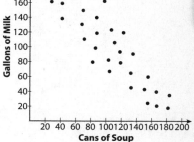

Hours Spent Reading vs. Pages Read

Milk Sold vs. Soup Sold

TRY IT OUT ➡ **Consider causation and correlation below.**

1   A team of scientists performs an experiment with the dolphins at an aquarium. They place a dolphin in a tank, release 50 fish, and record the number of fish that each dolphin catches in ten minutes.

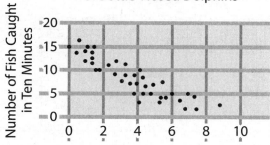

Effect of Captivity on Feeding Habits of Bottle-Nosed Dolphins

From their results, the scientists conclude that living in captivity causes bottle-nosed dolphins to lose their ability to catch fish effectively. Does the scientists' graph show correlation? _____

What are some other factors that could cause the correlation shown?

_____

_____

_____

Two-Way Frequency Tables

Sometimes data involves categories rather than numerical values. A two-way frequency table is useful for examining relationships with categorical variables. The frequency table shows how often a value occurs.

A two-way frequency table like the one below uses frequency counts. The table shows the hair and eye color of 100 dogs. Use the values that are known to fill in the values that are missing.

	Brown Fur	Black Fur	Yellow Fur	Gray Fur	TOTAL
Blue Eyes	10	5		25	40
Yellow Eyes	20	10	20		
TOTAL	30		20	35	100

Two-way tables can also show **relative frequencies** as a decimal (where 1 represents the whole sample set) or percent out of 100%. Use the information above to calculate the relative frequencies below.

	Brown Fur	Black Fur	Yellow Fur	Gray Fur	TOTAL
Blue Eyes	0.1 or 10%	0.05 or 5%	0.0 or 0%		
Yellow Eyes	0.2 or 20%	0.1 or 10%	0.20% or 20%		
TOTAL	0.3 or 30%	0.15 or 15%	0.2 or 20%		

The table above shows the relative frequency of the whole table. You can also show the relative frequency of the rows or the relative frequency of the columns. To find the relative frequency of a row (or column) divide the number for that variable by the total in that row (or column). For example, among blue-eyed dogs, the relative frequency of those who also have brown fur is $\frac{10}{40} = 0.25$ or 25%.

‖ TRY IT OUT ‖➡ **Use the data above to answer the questions.**

1. Among yellow-eyed dogs, _____ % have black fur.

2. Among black-furred dogs, _____ % have yellow eyes.

   On the lines below, explain why these two relative frequencies are different.

   _____

Combining Data with Two-Way Tables

You can use two-way tables to combine data categories using addition. You can also use addition to find the total number of members in a column, row, or table if it is not given.

▌TRY IT OUT▐ ➡ **Answer the questions below.**

2 Each student in 8th grade reports whether or not they have older or younger siblings. Their results are shown in the table below.

	Has an older sibling	**Does not have an older sibling**
Has a younger sibling	32	64
Does not have a younger sibling	51	42

How many students are only children? _____

How many total students have an older sibling? _____

How many students are either the youngest or the oldest in their families but are not only children? _____

What percent of students who have older siblings also have younger siblings? _____

What percent of students who have younger siblings also have older siblings? _____

What percent of the total students in the survey are middle children?
_____

Independent Practice

Use the 4-Step Method for Problem Solving and the strategies you have learned in this lesson to solve the problems in this section.

Use the information below to answer questions 1 and 2.

The two-way frequency table below shows the movie preferences of 100 middle school students and parents.

	Comedy	Drama	Science Fiction	Adventure	TOTAL
Parents	5	15	0	10	30
Students	30	5	15	20	70
TOTAL	35	20	15	30	100

1 What is the relative frequency of people who prefer dramas?

A .05

B .15

C .2

D 20

hint ▶ *Relative frequencies use 1 to represent the whole sample.*

2 Among parents, what percent prefer adventure movies?

A 3%

B 10%

C 30%

D 33%

hint ▶ *First identify the total number of parents.*

3 Evaluate the statement below.

In the past 50 years, obesity rates and pollution in the atmosphere have both increased. Therefore, pollution in the atmosphere causes obesity.

A Both obesity and pollution have been increasing, so this is a causal relationship.

B Both obesity and pollution have been increasing, but obesity rates are the cause of increased pollution in the atmosphere.

C Although there is a correlation between obesity and pollution, it could be caused by a third variable such as increased use of cars.

D Although there is a correlation between obesity and pollution, it is not possible to do research on this relationship.

hint *Remember that correlation does not imply causation. In all studies, it is important to look for other factors.*

4 A group of scientists is studying the impact of cutting down or burning areas in a rainforest ecosystem. They show their results on the graph below.

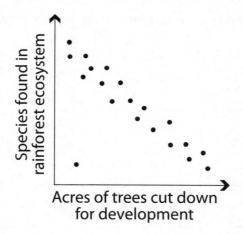

The scientists notice that there is an outlier in their data. What should their next steps be to address the outlier?

A Change the data point to match their other data.

B Ignore the outlier because it probably is not important.

C Investigate the area that produced the data to see what other factors are involved.

D Start their research project over again from the beginning to look for different relationships.

hint *Outliers in a data set should never be ignored—always check the data collection method, the resource that produced the data, and other factors that may impact the data.*

5 A school records the number of students in each grade whose typing speed is higher or lower than 30 words per minute, as shown below.

	Grade 6	Grade 7	Grade 8
Typing Speed Above 30 Words per Minute	16	88	98
Typing Speed Below 30 Words per Minute	97	20	7

What percent of 7th grade students can type over 30 words per minute?

Answer _____

What percent of the students who can type over 30 words per minute are in 8th grade?

Answer _____

On the lines below, describe a trend that is present in the table and explain why it might occur.

_____

_____

_____

_____

hint ▷ *Notice how the data changes along the rows and down the columns to find the trend.*

6 Ms. Bali made the scatter plot below to show the number of hours each student worked on an assigned project and the grade the student received.

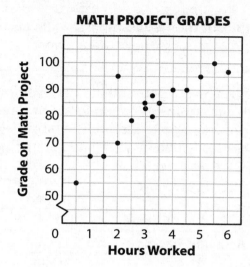

MATH PROJECT GRADES

Circle any clusters in the scatter plot. Put a box around any outliers in the scatter plot.

On the lines below, explain the circumstances that might have caused the cluster.

_____

_____

_____

On the lines below, explain the circumstances that might have caused the outlier.

_____

_____

_____

hint *Think about how students in your class work on assignments and the grades they receive. How are those relationships represented in the chart?*

KAP Wrap

Read the question and sample student answer below. Then, use the rubric on page 24 to score the student's work.

---

1 A visa is a permit that the government issues to allow foreign citizens to either immigrate or stay for an extended period to work or go to school. The table below shows the number of visas issued by the United States in one year.

	Immigrant Visas Issued	Non-Immigrant Visas Issued
Africa	39,181	205,365
East Asia and Pacific	113,647	1,433,500
Europe	41,553	933,522
South and Central Asia	60,419	549,421
Western Hemisphere	197,709	2,890,372

Approximately how many non-immigrant visas were issued in one year?

Show your work.

$200,000 + 1,400,000 + 900,000 + 500,000$

$+ 2,900,000 = 5,900,000$

Answer   5,900,000

Approximately what percentage of visas issued to African citizens are immigrant visas?

Show your work.

$40,000 \div 200,000 = .2$ or 20%

Answer   20%

I would give this student a _____ out of 3 because _____

_____

_____

_____

UNIT 5 Strategies for Geometry

Lesson 1
TRANSFORMING AND COMPARING SHAPES

Focus Question

How can you identify and create congruent and similar shapes?

Thinking KAP

Three students are playing a math game. Callie and Naomi describe a triangle using sides and angles. Then, Rebecca identifies the triangle they describe.

Callie believes that she can give Rebecca all of the information she needs to find a specific triangle by just telling her the measure of the three angles. Naomi believes that she should give her the measure of the three sides instead.

Who is correct, and why?

_____

_____

_____

_____

Instruction

Transformations

The chart below reviews three types of transformations. When a figure is transformed, the new figure is called the **image**.

TRY IT OUT **Fill in the names for the transformations and describe how each figure was transformed.**

Transformation	Example
A ______________ is a flip over a line. The diagram shows ____________________ ____.	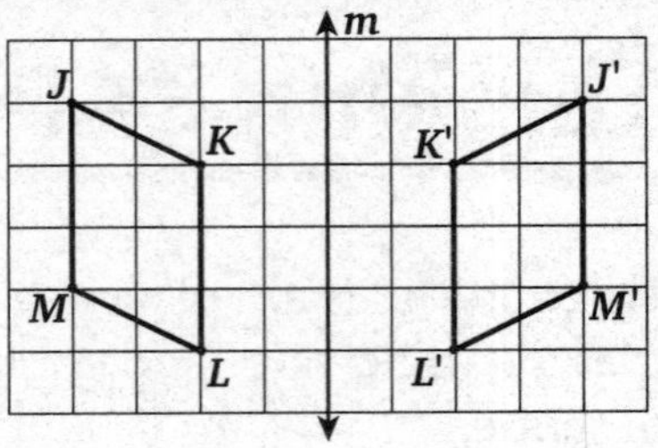
A ______________ is a slide of an object a certain number of units to a new location. The diagram shows ____________________ ____ ____.	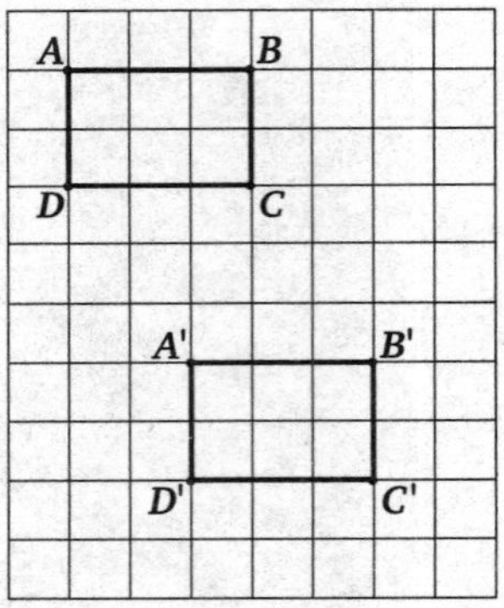
A ____________ is a turn around a point. The diagram shows ____________________ ____ ____.	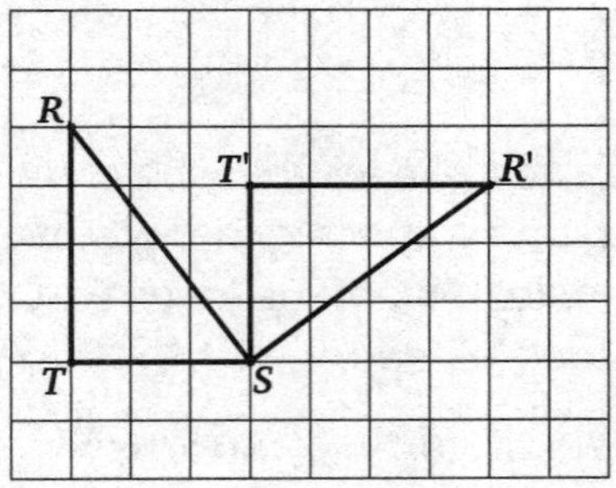

Congruence

Think of **congruent** shapes like copies from a photocopier. To prove that two shapes are congruent, match these parts:

- match lines to lines and segments to segments of the same length
- match angles to angles with the same angle measure
- match parallel lines to parallel lines

TRY IT OUT ➡ **Determine if the triangles are congruent.**

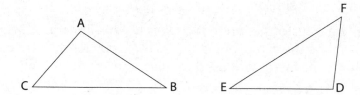

Which line segment corresponds to side BC? _____
Compare lengths.

Which angle corresponds to ∠FED? _____
Compare angle measures.

Check each of the remaining sides and angles. Are they congruent? _____

Postulates for Congruent Triangles

If you can prove that a few parts of a triangle are congruent, they may prove all of the other parts to be congruent.

- **Side-side-side (SSS):** If all corresponding sides are congruent, the triangles are congruent.
- **Side-angle-side (SAS):** If two sides and the angle *between them* are congruent, the triangles are congruent.
- **Angle-side-angle (ASA)** or **angle-angle-side (AAS):** If two corresponding angles and one corresponding side are congruent, the triangles are congruent.

TRY IT OUT ➡ **Determine if each set of triangles is congruent.**

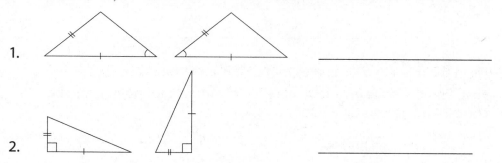

1. _____

2. _____

Similar Shapes and Dilations

Similar shapes have congruent angles that appear in the same order. Because their angles are the same, their sides must be proportionate to each other. Think of similar shapes as photocopies that have been scaled up or down. There is one postulate for similar triangles:

- **Angle-angle-angle (AAA):** If all corresponding angles are congruent, the triangles are similar.

A **dilation** is a transformation that creates a similar image. It keeps the angles in a shape the same, but changes their side lengths by a **scale factor**. What scale factor was used to make the image below?

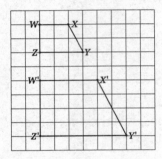

_____

To dilate a figure, multiply each coordinate by the given scale factor. Then, use those coordinates to draw and label the image.

‖ TRY IT OUT ‖ ➡ **Solve the problem below.**

1   The table below shows the coordinates of triangle ABC and the coordinate of A′ in triangle A′B′C′. Triangle A′B′C′ is a dilation of triangle ABC.

Triangle ABC		Triangle A′B′C′	
A	(1, −4)	A′	(2, −8)
B	(3, 1)	B′	
C	(5, −4)	C′	

Fill in the missing coordinates for point B′ and point C′.

First, find the scale factor. Divide each coordinate for point A′ by the corresponding coordinate for point A.

$$\frac{2}{1} = \underline{\quad} \text{ and } \frac{-8}{-4} = \underline{\quad}$$

Now, multiply each coordinate of the other two points by the scale factor.

Proving Congruence through Transformations

Another way to show that two shapes are congruent is to list the transformations that were used to make the image. Reflections, rotations, and translations create congruent images. Dilations create similar images.

When you describe transformations, be specific. For example, an image might be *reflected horizontally, rotated 90° clockwise, translated 4 units to the left,* and *scaled up by a factor of 2.*

Transformations on a Coordinate Grid

To **reflect a point over the x-axis**, keep the x-coordinates the same and change the sign of the y-coordinates. To **reflect a point over the y-axis**, keep the y-coordinates the same and change the sign of the x-coordinates.

To **rotate a point around the origin by 90°**, switch the order of the x- and y-coordinates. Then, check the quadrant to give each one the appropriate sign.

TRY IT OUT ➡ **Use a table to transform the shape in the problem below.**

Transform shape ABCDEF by scaling it down by a factor of 2, reflecting it over the x-axis, rotating it 90° counterclockwise, then translating it 3 units to the right.

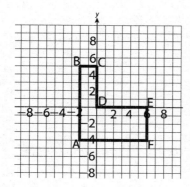 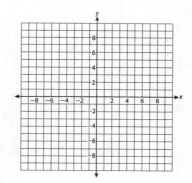

	A	B	C	D	E	F
Original	(−2, −4)					
Dilation						
Reflection						
Rotation						
Translation						

When you are finished, plot the points. Does your answer make sense? _____

Independent Practice

Use the 4-Step Method for Problem Solving and the strategies you have learned in this lesson to solve the problems in this section.

1 Monica drew a triangle on the coordinate grid shown below.

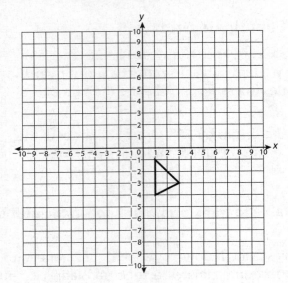

If Monica reflects the triangle across the *x*-axis, what will be the new coordinates of the vertices of the triangle?

A (−1, −1), (−3, −3), (−1, −4)

B (−1, 1), (−3, 3), (−1, 4)

C (1, 1), (3, 3), (1, 4)

D (−1, −1), (−3, 3), (1, 4)

hint ▸ *Draw the reflection. Then, match the coordinates of each vertex to the answer choices.*

2   Two congruent triangles are shown below.

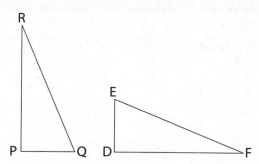

Which set of instructions describes how triangle PQR was transformed into DEF?

A   rotate 90° clockwise, translate to the right

B   reflect over a horizontal line, rotate 90° clockwise, translate to the right

C   reflect over a vertical line, rotate 90° counterclockwise, translate to the right

D   reflect over a horizontal line, rotate 90° counterclockwise, translate to the right

hint   *Mark the corresponding sides of the triangles. Then try each set of instructions.*

3   The diagram below shows two slides. The slides form similar triangles.

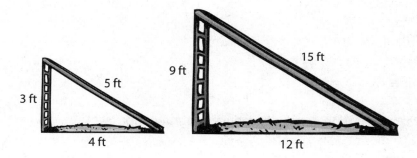

Which fraction represents the ratio of the measures of the smaller slide to the measures of the larger slide?

A $\frac{1}{5}$

B $\frac{1}{4}$

C $\frac{1}{3}$

D $\frac{4}{5}$

hint   *All of the sides are in the same proportion, so you can choose any pair of corresponding sides to set up the ratio.*

4 Two triangles are shown below.

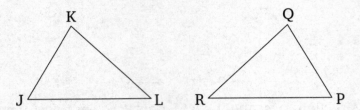

Which set of relationships proves that the triangles are congruent?

A ∠KJL ≅ ∠QPR, ∠KLJ ≅ ∠QRP, ∠JKL ≅ ∠QPR

B $\overline{JK}$ ≅ $\overline{PQ}$, ∠LKJ ≅ ∠RQP, ∠KLJ ≅ ∠QRP

C $\overline{JK}$ ≅ $\overline{PQ}$, $\overline{JL}$ ≅ $\overline{PR}$, ∠KLJ ≅ ∠QRP

D $\overline{LK}$ ≅ $\overline{RQ}$, $\overline{JL}$ ≅ $\overline{PR}$, ∠LKJ ≅ ∠RQP

5 The perimeter of rectangle JKLM is 20 centimeters. Under which transformation could the perimeter of the image, rectangle J'K'L'M', be less than 20 centimeters?

A dilation

B reflection

C rotation

D translation

hint ▶ *Which transformation does not produce congruent figures?*

6   Juan drew triangle DEF on the grid below.

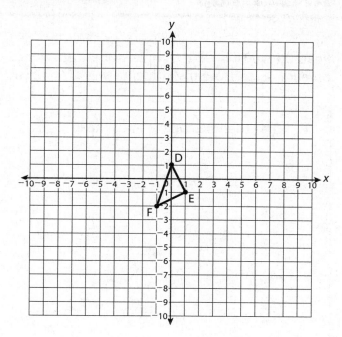

He wants to draw triangle D'E'F', a dilation of triangle DEF with a scale factor of 3 and rotation 90° clockwise around the origin. What are the coordinates of point D', point E', and point F'?

Answer D' = (_____ , _____)

    E' = (_____ , _____)

    F' = (_____ , _____)

On the grid above, draw triangle D'E'F'.

hint   *Use a table to keep track of each point. Then, use the new coordinates to draw the image.*

KAP Wrap

Read the question and sample student answer below. Then, use the rubric on page 25 to score the student's work.

1 The triangles below are similar.

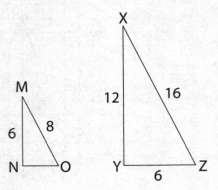

What fraction represents the ratio of the lengths of the sides of the small triangle to the lengths of the sides of the large triangle?

Show your work.

	MN:XZ	Simplify
MNO	6	3
XYZ	16	8

Answer _____ $\frac{3}{8}$ _____

I would give this student a _____ out of 2, because _____

_____

_____

_____

2 Lesson 2
TRIANGLES

Focus Question
How can you find the missing side lengths and angle measures in a triangle?

Thinking KAP

Khalid needs to travel between the points marked on the map with stars. The long blocks on the map are 40 meters long and the shorter blocks are 30 meters long.

If Khalid followed the streets, how far would he walk?

_____ meters

If Khalid cuts diagonally through the grassy field behind the buildings, how far would he walk?

_____ meters

How much shorter is the diagonal path? _____ meters

Instruction

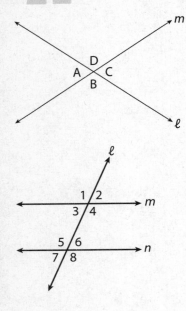

Angle Measures

When the sum of two angles is 180° they are **supplementary** and can make a straight line. When the sum of two angles is 90°, they are **complementary** and can make a right angle.

When two lines intersect, they form two pairs of congruent, **vertical angles**. When two parallel lines are intersected by a **transversal**, they form eight angles.

In each diagram on the left, identify each set of congruent angles with a special mark.

If ∠A measures 70°, what is the measure of ∠B? _____

If ∠4 is 135°, what is the measure of ∠5? _____

Angles in Triangles

The angles inside a shape are **interior angles**. You can use transversals to prove the sum of the interior angles in a triangle.

To begin, draw a triangle, XYZ. Then, draw a line, *s*, that is parallel to one of its sides and which intersects its opposite vertex. You now have two parallel lines intersected by two transversals.

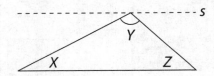

Using transversals, label the angle congruent to ∠X. Repeat with ∠Z.

Using angles along line *s*, what is the sum of the angle measures of X, Y, and Z? _____

Therefore, the sum of the interior angles in a triangle is _____.

You should also memorize that the sum of the interior angles in a quadrilateral is 360°. You can remember that each angle in a square is 90° and there are 4 angles.

▌TRII T OUT▐ ➡ Solve the problem below.

1 Nina drew a triangle that had a 50° angle and a 30° angle. What is the measure of the third angle in the triangle?

A 10°	**C** 100°
B 60°	**D** 280°

Which choice can you eliminate immediately? _____

The Pythagorean Theorem

The Pythagorean theorem shows the relationship between the sides in a right triangle. The two **legs** are the sides by the right angle, represented by a and b. The **hypotenuse** is across from the right angle, represented by c.

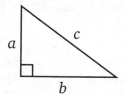

$$a^2 + b^2 = c^2$$

▌TRIP IT OUT▐ ➡ **Use the Pythagorean theorem.**

2 Triangle ABC is shown below. What is the length of $\overline{BC}$?

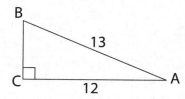

A 1	**C** 5
B 4	**D** 11

Which variable should you use for 12? _____ For 13? _____

Substitute the numbers into the Pythagorean theorem and solve.

Pythagorean Triples

The square roots of most whole numbers are irrational. A **Pythagorean triple** is a set of three whole numbers that can make a right triangle. One of these is the 5-12-13 triangle above. Memorize these Pythagorean triples.

3-4-5 **5-12-13** **7-24-25** **8-15-17**

Pythagorean triples may also appear in their multiples. For example, $3^2 + 4^2 = 5^2$ so you also know that $6^2 + 8^2 = 10^2$ and $9^2 + 12^2 = 15^2$.

▌TRY IT OUT▐ ➡ **Use Pythagorean triples to solve the problem.**

3 A right triangle has legs with lengths 16 and 30. What is the length of its hypotenuse?

A 32	**C** 39
B 34	**D** 41

Proving the Pythagorean Theorem

There are many **proofs** of the Pythagorean theorem available. The one below is the one that Pythagoras used.

Step 1 Draw any right triangle.

Step 2 Draw the squares of each side. Remember, when you say "*a* squared" you're talking about the area of a square with side lengths of *a*!

Step 3 Using congruent shapes, you can make two squares that each have a side length of *a* + *b*. Squares with the same side lengths are congruent.

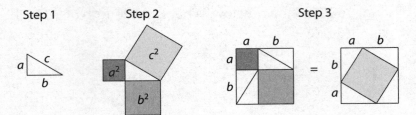

Step 1 Step 2 Step 3

Step 4 Using the Additive Property of Equality, you can subtract the same amount from both sides of an equation and still have equal amounts on both sides. Subtract the area of 4 triangles from each side.

Step 5 Write the equation showing the amounts on each side of the equation.

The Converse

The **converse**, or reverse order, of the Pythagorean theorem is that if a triangle has the relationship $a^2 + b^2 = c^2$ between its sides, it must be a right triangle.

▌TRY IT OUT▌➡ **Use the converse of the Pythagorean theorem to solve the problem.**

4   Nadia drew the triangle below. Is Nadia's triangle a right triangle?

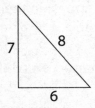

Substitute the numbers into the Pythagorean theorem to determine whether Nadia has drawn a right triangle.

Explain why the triangle is or is not a right triangle.

Distances between Points

You can use the Pythagorean theorem to find the distance between two points on a coordinate grid. Use the two points as the endpoints of the hypotenuse, then draw the legs to form a right triangle. Follow the steps below to find the distance between points M and K in the grid below.

Step 1 Plot a point at (2, 2) and label it J.

Step 2 Draw triangle JKM.

Step 3 The length of $\overline{JK}$ = _____

The length of $\overline{JM}$ = _____

Step 4 Use the Pythagorean theorem to find the length of $\overline{MK}$

_____

The length of $\overline{MK}$ = _____

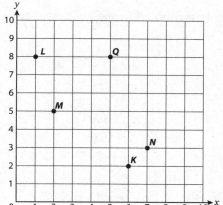

If the length of a side is an irrational number, remember to express it with the square root sign unless you are asked for an approximation.

❚ TRY IT OUT ❚➡ **Find the distance between each pair of points on the grid above.**

1. L and N _____

2. Q and M _____

3. K and N _____

4. What is the perimeter of triangle LQM? _____

Independent Practice

Use the 4-Step Method for Problem Solving and the strategies you have learned in this lesson to solve the problems in this section.

1   Rectangle WXYZ is formed by triangle ZWX and triangle XYZ, as shown below.

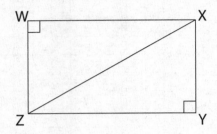

If WZ = 4 and YZ = 6, what is the length of ZX?

A $\sqrt{10}$

B   7

C $\sqrt{52}$

D $\sqrt{61}$

hint   *What do you know about parallel sides in a rectangle?*

2   What is the measure of angle O in the figure below?

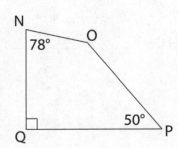

A   102°

B   142°

C   172°

D   232°

hint   *Angle Q is a right angle, which means it measures 90°.*

3 Triangle DEF is shown below.

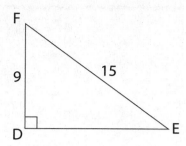

What is the length of $\overline{DE}$?

A 6

B 12

C 14

D 24

hint ▷ *Can you use Pythagorean triples?*

4 Two points are shown on the grid below.

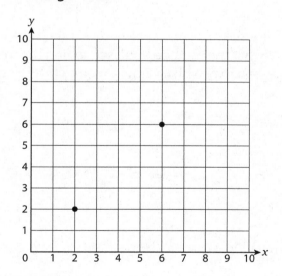

What is the distance between the two points?

A 4

B $\sqrt{32}$

C 8

D $\sqrt{128}$

hint ▷ *Draw a right triangle with the distance between the points as the hypotenuse.*

5 Triangle DEF is shown below.

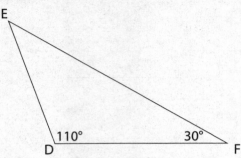

What is the measure of ∠DEF?

Answer _____ °

On the lines below, explain how you can determine the measure of the angle without using a protractor.

_____

_____

In the space below, prove that the method you used to find the missing angle measure is mathematically accurate. You may wish to draw a picture in addition to explaining your steps.

_____

_____

_____

_____

hint ▷ *Start by drawing a line parallel to $\overline{DF}$. Explain how you know the relationship between each set of angles.*

6 Stephen drew the triangle below.

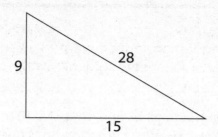

Is Stephen's triangle a right triangle? Use the Pythagorean theorem to prove whether or not his triangle is a right triangle.

Show your work.

Answer _____

On the lines below, explain how you know your answer is correct.

_____

_____

_____

_____

_____

hint ▶ *Use Say It! Support It!*

KAP Wrap

Read the question and sample student answer below. Then, use the rubric on page 25 to score the student's work.

---

1 In triangle LMN below, LM is 10 meters long and MN is 7 meters long. Use the Pythagorean theorem to find the length of $\overline{LN}$ to the nearest tenth of a meter.

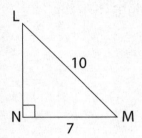

Show your work.

$c^2 = 7^2 + 10^2$

$c^2 = 49 + 100$

$c^2 = 149$

$c \approx 12.2$

Answer _____12.2_____ meters

I would give this student a _____ out of 2, because _____

_____

_____

3

Lesson 3
SOLIDS AND MULTI-STEP PROBLEMS

Focus Question
What strategies can you use to solve problems with area and volume?

Thinking KAP

David is getting ready for his soccer game. His job is to fill up a water cooler with a radius of 6 inches and a height of 20 inches. He is using a pitcher that has a radius of 3 inches and a height of 10 inches.

How much water can the water cooler hold? _____ cubic inches

How much water can the pitcher hold? _____ cubic inches

How many full pitchers will David need to fill the water cooler? _____

Volume of a Cylinder

To find the volume of a cylinder, start with what you already know.

Area and Circumference of a Circle

The area and circumference of a circle are determined by the radius.

A = πr^2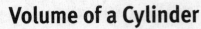

C = $\pi \cdot d$

Volume of Prisms

A **prism** has two polygon bases. All of its other faces are rectangles. The volume of any prism is the area of the base multiplied by the height.

❚TRY IT OUT❚ ➡ **Write the formula, then find the volume of each prism below.**

6 in. 5 in. 4 in.

10 cm 25 cm 8 cm

V = $l \cdot w \cdot h$

V = 120 cu. in.

V = Area of triangle • height

V = 1000 cu. cm

Volume of a Cylinder

A **cylinder** has two circular bases. To find the volume of any solid that has the same area throughout the height of the shape, you can multiply the area of the base by the height. Thus, the formula for the volume of a cylinder is

$$V = \pi r^2 h$$

❚TRY IT OUT❚ ➡ **Find the volume of the cylinder.**

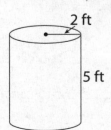

2 ft

5 ft

V = 20π cubic feet

Volumes of Cones and Spheres

Pyramids have one polygon base and their other sides are triangles that meet at a point. **Cones** have one circular base and a curved surface that meets at a point.

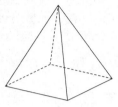

$$V = \frac{1}{3}\, bh$$

$$V = \frac{1}{3}\, \pi r^2 h$$

Compare the formulas for the volume of a square pyramid and a cone.

_____

_____

Spheres are composed of all of the points that are the distance of the radius from their centers.

The volume of a sphere is $V = \frac{4}{3}\, \pi r^3$

When making calculations with π and cube roots, remember to always keep your answers in those terms unless you are asked to give an approximation.

▌TRY IT OUT▌ ➡ **Use the formula to solve the problem below.**

1 Ty has a beach ball shaped like a globe, as shown below. It has a diameter of 24 inches.

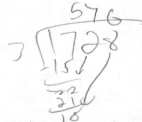

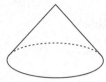

What is the volume of air that is needed to inflate the beach ball?

- **A** 1,296π cubic inches
- **B** 1,728π cubic inches
- **C** 2,304π cubic inches
- **D** 18,432π cubic inches

Two-Step Problems

The key to all problems with circles, cylinders, spheres, and cones is the radius. In any two-step problem with these shapes, always use what you are given to *find the radius*. Then, use the radius to find the other value.

▌TRY IT OUT▐ ➡ **Solve the problem below by finding the radius.**

2 Triangle PQR is inscribed in circle O, as shown below.

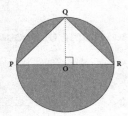

If the area of circle O is 16π, what is the length of $\overline{QR}$?

Use the area to find the radius. *r* = _____

How can you use the radius to find the length of $\overline{QR}$?

_____

_____

Solve the problem. $\overline{QR}$ = _____

To solve problems with prisms, you will often need to use one hypotenuse to find another hypotenuse.

▌TRY IT OUT▐ ➡ **Use two hypotenuses to solve the problem below.**

3 What is the distance between points X and Y in the cube below?

First, imagine a right triangle that uses X and Y for two of its points. Draw point Z at the bottom right vertex of the front square. Then, draw triangle XYZ.

Think of $\overline{XZ}$ as the hypotenuse of a triangle on the front of the cube. Use the Pythagorean theorem to find the length of $\overline{XZ}$.

_____

Now, think of $\overline{XZ}$ and $\overline{YZ}$ as the legs of another triangle to find the length of $\overline{XY}$.

_____

Drawing a Picture

Some geometry problems will give you a description of a shape in words only. Draw a picture to solve these problems. You may want to practice drawing some basic shapes like cubes, cylinders, pyramids, and spheres.

▌TRY IT OUT▌➡ **Draw a picture to help you solve this problem.**

A can of soup completely fills a cylinder 5 inches tall and 3 inches in diameter. If one can of soup is poured into a cylindrical pot with a diameter of 6 inches, to what depth, in inches, will it fill the pot?

    A 1.25   **C** 2.5

    B 2   **D** 5

Which answer choice can you eliminate? Why?

_____

_____

Draw a picture to represent the information in the problem.

What do you know? _____

_____

What do you need? _____

How can you use what you know to find what you need?

_____

_____

_____

Solve the problem.

Independent Practice

Use the 4-Step Method for Problem Solving and the strategies you have learned in this lesson to solve the problems in this section.

1 A cylinder is shown below.

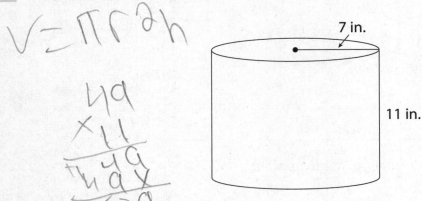

$V = \pi r^2 h$

49
$\times 11$
$\overline{49}$
$49x$
$\overline{539}$

7 in.

11 in.

What is the volume of the cylinder?

A 77π cubic inches

B 231π cubic inches

C 539π cubic inches

D $1,078\pi$ cubic inches

hint ▸ *The volume of any shape that is the same width throughout is the area of the base times the height.*

2 A cone has a base with a circumference of 16π and a height of 6. What is the volume of the cone?

A 128π

B 512π

C 384π

D $1,536\pi$

$V = \frac{1}{3}\pi r^2 h$

hint ▸ *Draw and label a sketch. Then, find the radius before moving to the second step.*

3 A sphere has a volume of 36π. What is the radius of the sphere?

A 2

B 3

C 4

D 5

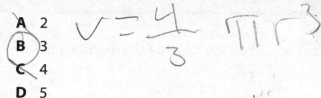

hint Use Backsolving. Write the formula for the volume of a sphere, then fill in each answer choice for the radius.

4 A cube is cut in half along its diagonal to form a triangular prism.

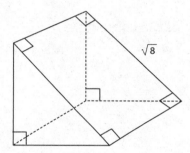

$\sqrt{8}$

What is the volume of the triangular prism, in cubic units?

A 2

B 4

C 8

D 16

hint The solid started out as a square, so both legs are the same length. You can write the Pythagorean theorem with $a^2 + a^2 = c^2$ to find the missing side lengths. What value of a will make the equation true?

5 A company is choosing a container for a new cereal. The containers are shown below.

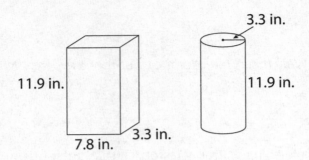

3.3 in.

11.9 in.

11.9 in.

7.8 in.   3.3 in.

[not drawn to scale]

Estimate the volume of each of the containers.

Show your work.

72 X 8 X 3   106   ×3/9

12   96   ×3
×8   ×3
96   28

288   18
×3
324

Estimated volume of prism _____288_____ cubic inches

Estimated volume of cylinder _____324_____ cubic inches

The company wants to use the container that holds the most cereal. Which container should they choose?

Answer ____Cylender____

hint ▷ *You can round the values before putting them in the formulas. This will make the estimates less accurate, so this is only a good idea if the volumes are far apart.*

6 A circle is inscribed in a square, which means that each side of the square touches the circle at exactly one point.

If the area of the circle is 144π, what is the length of diagonal $\overline{DB}$?

Show your work.

$144 \ \pi r^2$

$12 \times 2 = 24$

$C = ^2 24^2 + 24^2$

$C = 1152$

$\sqrt{1152}$

Answer _164_

On the lines below, explain the steps you took to find your answer.

I calculated Pi times the radius² and I got 1152 and after finding the square rute of that I got my answer 164

hint What is the relationship between a radius of the circle and the length of one side of the square?

KAP Wrap

Read the question and sample student answer below. Then, use the rubric on page 25 to score the student's work.

---

1 Sina draws a picture of a cylinder as shown below.

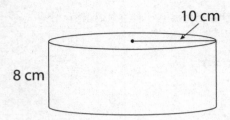

[not drawn to scale]

Calculate the volume of Sina's cylinder to the nearest whole number.

Show your work.

(3.14)(8)^2(10) = V

(3.14)(64)(10) = 2,009.6

Answer ____2,010____ cubic centimeters

I would give this student a _____ out of 2, because _____

_____

_____

_____

GLOSSARY

Number Names

Whole Numbers

Number	English Name	Nombre en Español
1	one	uno
2	two	dos
3	three	tres
4	four	cuatro
5	five	cinco
6	six	seis
7	seven	siete
8	eight	ocho
9	nine	nueve
10	ten	diez
11	eleven	once
12	twelve	doce
13	thirteen	trece
14	fourteen	catorce
15	fifteen	quince
16	sixteen	diez y seis
17	seventeen	diez y siete
18	eighteen	diez y ocho
19	nineteen	diez y nueve
20	twenty	veinte

Number	English Name	Nombre en Español
21	twenty-one	veinte y uno
22	twenty-two	veinte y dos
23	twenty-three	veinte y tres
24	twenty-four	veinte y cuatro
25	twenty-five	veinte y cinco
26	twenty-six	veinte y seis
27	twenty-seven	veinte y siete
28	twenty-eight	veinte y ocho
29	twenty-nine	veinte y nueve
30	thirty	treinta
40	forty	cuaranta
50	fifty	cinquenta
60	sixty	sesenta
70	seventy	setenta
80	eighty	ochenta
90	ninety	noventa
100	one hundred	cién
1,000	one thousand	mil
100,000	one hundred thousand	cien miles
1,000,000	one million	millión

Fractions

Number	Diagram	English Name	Nombre en Español
$\frac{1}{2}$		one-half	un medio
$\frac{1}{3}$		one-third	un tercio
$\frac{1}{4}$		one-fourth	un cuarto
$\frac{1}{5}$		one-fifth	un quinto
$\frac{1}{6}$		one-sixth	un sexto
$\frac{1}{8}$		one-eighth	un octavo
$\frac{1}{10}$		one-tenth	un décimo

Glossary

A

acute angle (*el ángulo agudo*) An angle which measures between 0° and 90°.

acute triangle (*el triángulo agudo*) A triangle with three acute angles. An acute angle measures between 0° and 90°.

additive inverse (*el inverso aditivo*) A number which, when added to another number, results in a sum of 0. For example, $6 + (-6) = 0$, therefore, -6 is the additive inverse of 6.

adjacent (*adyacente*) Next to or beside. For example, $\angle AEC$ and $\angle CEB$ are adjacent because they lie next to each other.

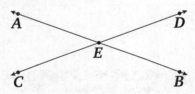

adjacent side of a triangle (*el lado adyacente del triángulo*) Two sides which are next to or beside each other. Any two sides of a triangle are adjacent because each side touches or lies next to the other two sides.

algebra (*el algebra*) The area of mathematics that involves writing math statements in a general way. In algebra, unknown numbers are called *variables* and are represented by letters. For example, 4 less than a number, x, is written as $x - 4$.

algebraic equation (*una ecuación algebraica*) A number sentence written using numbers, variables, and an equal sign. Usually, the number sentence also includes one or more operations. For example, $3x + 5 = 35$ and $x = 10$ are algebraic equations.

algebraic expression (*una expresión algebraica*) A quantity written using numbers and variables. This may or may not contain operations, but will not contain a relation symbol. For example, x, $x + 7$, and $3x$ are algebraic expressions.

algebraic inequality (*una desigualdad algebraica*) A number sentence that is written using numbers, variables, and symbols such as $>$ (greater than), $\geq$ (greater than or equal to), $<$ (less than), and $\leq$ (less than or equal to) to compare values. For example, $12 > 2n - 4$ is an algebraic inequality.

algebraic patterns (*unas configuraciones alegbraicas*) An arrangement of numbers that follow a rule. For example, the two groups of numbers below follow the algebraic pattern "multiply by 2." The numbers in Column 2 are twice the numbers in Column 1.

Column 1	Column 2
2	4
3	6
4	8
5	10
6	12

The pattern is "multiply by 2."

algebraic relationship (una relación algebraica)
Two sets of numbers have an algebraic relationship if the numbers follow a rule such as "add 1," "multiply by 3," or "divide by 2." For example, the two groups of numbers below have an algebraic relationship because they follow the rule "divide by 2." Each number in Column 2 is half of the number in Column 1.

Column 1	Column 2
2	1
4	2
6	3
8	4
10	5

The relationship is "divide by 2."

algebraic solution (una solución algebraica) The number or set of numbers that satisfies an equation or inequality. For example, the algebraic solution to the equation $x + 4 = 5$ is $x = 1$.

algebraically (algebraico) A problem is expressed algebraically if it contains numbers, variables, and operation symbols such as $+$, $-$, $\div$, and $\times$.

alternate exterior angles (ángulos alternos exteriores) When parallel lines are cut by a transversal, the angles outside of the parallel lines and on opposite sides of the transversal are called *alternate exterior angles*. These angles are congruent. In the diagram, $\angle 1$ and $\angle 8$, and $\angle 2$ and $\angle 7$, are alternate exterior angles.

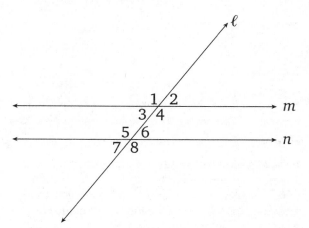

alternate interior angles (ángulos alternos interiores) When parallel lines are cut by a transversal, angles between the parallel lines and on opposite sides of the transversal are called *alternate interior angles*. These angles are congruent. In the diagram, $\angle 3$ and $\angle 6$, and $\angle 4$ and $\angle 5$, are alternate interior angles.

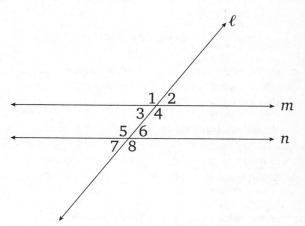

altitude (la altitud) A line segment that extends from a vertex of a figure and meets the base opposite it at a right angle. Altitude can also be called the *height*. In the diagram, the altitude measures 6 centimeters.

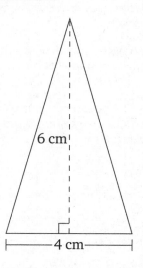

6 cm

4 cm

analog clock (un reloj análogo) A timepiece that has hour and minute hands.

GLOSSARY

angle (*el ángulo*) A figure formed by two rays with a common endpoint. The common endpoint is called the *vertex* of the angle.

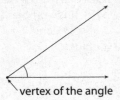

vertex of the angle

angle bisector (*un bisectriz de un ángulo*) A ray, line, or line segment that divides an angle into two smaller, congruent angles.

angle pairs (*pares de ángulos*) A pair of angles formed by the intersection of two or more lines that share a special relationship such as vertical angles, alternate interior angles, alternate exterior angles, or corresponding angles.

ante meridian, A.M. (*antes del medio día*) The label given to the hours between 12:00 midnight and 12:00 noon. It describes the morning hours. For example, 8:00 A.M. is 8 o'clock in the morning.

approximation (*una aproximación*) The process of estimating a solution to a problem using mathematical strategies. Rounding numbers is one way to approximate.

arc (*un arco*) A part of a circle that consists of all the points between two endpoints on the circumference of the circle.

area (*el area*) The number of square units needed to cover a flat region. For example, the area of the rectangle shown is 8 square feet.

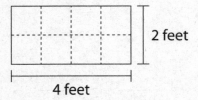

2 feet

4 feet

Area = 8 square feet

arithmetic expression (*una expresión aritmética*) A combination of numbers with one or more arithmetic operations. For example, $3 + 2$, and $(8 - 3) \div 5$.

arithmetically (*aritmético*) A problem is written or solved arithmetically if numbers and operation symbols such as $+$, $-$, $\times$, and $\div$ are used.

array (*una serie, una colección, un grupo*) A rectangular arrangement of objects in equal rows or columns.

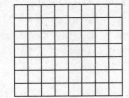

associative property (*la propiedad asociativa*) The order in which you group numbers does not change the sum or product. For example, $(2 + 4) + 6 = 2 + (4 + 6)$ and $(2 \times 4) \times 6 = 2 \times (4 \times 6)$.

attribute (*un atributo*) A property or quality of a number or object. For example, three attributes of the number 16 are that it is even, a multiple of 8, and a square number.

axis (*el eje*) The vertical and horizontal lines that divide the coordinate plane into quadrants. The horizontal axis is the *x*-axis, and the vertical axis is the *y*-axis. The plural is "axes" (*los ejes*).

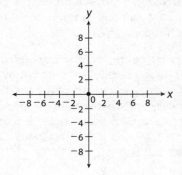

B

bar graph (*una gráfica de barra*) A graph that uses vertical or horizontal bars to indicate relationships among data.

base of a percent (*la base de un porcentaje*) The number considered to be the whole amount when calculating a percentage. It typically appears after the word "of" in a percentage problem. For example, in the problem "What percent of 15 is 5?", the base is 15.

base of a three-dimensional shape (*la base de una figura tridimensional*) A face to which an altitude is perpendicular. The base of the pyramid shown is a square.

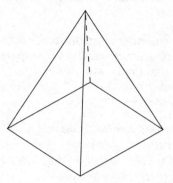

base of a two-dimensional shape (*la base de una figura de dos dimensiones*) A side of a geometric figure to which an altitude is perpendicular. In the diagram, the base measures 4 centimeters.

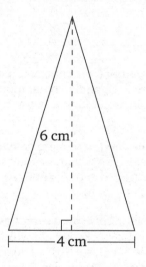

6 cm

4 cm

base-ten number system (*el sistema de numeración de la base diez*) The number system that uses place values such as ones, tens, hundreds, thousands, etc., to the left of the decimal point. It uses tenths, hundredths, thousandths, etc., to the right of the decimal point.

binomial (*binomio*) In algebra, an expression consisting of the sum or difference of two monomials, such as $4a - 8b$.

bisector (*bisectriz*) A ray, line, plane, or line segment which divides an angle or line segment into two congruent angles or line segments.

C

calculate (*calcular*) To add, subtract, multiply, and divide numbers.

calendar (*el calendario*) A chart used to keep track of dates. One year has 12 months. With the exception of February, each month has 30 or 31 days.

capacity (*la capacidad*) The amount of space in a container such as a box or a bottle. For example, if a bottle contains 12 ounces of water, then the capacity of the bottle is 12 ounces.

Celsius (*gradio Celsius*) A scale for measuring temperature. Degrees Celsius is written using the symbol °C. Water freezes at 0°C and boils at 100°C.

centimeter (*un centímetro*) A unit of length in the metric system, abbreviated as "cm". There are 100 centimeters in 1 meter.

central angle (*ángulo central*) An angle that has its vertex at the center of a circle. The measure of the central angle equals the measure of the arc (the portion of the circle which lies within the angle).

chord (*cuerda*) A line segment whose endpoints lie on a circle.

circle (*un círculo*) The set of all points on a flat surface that are the same distance from the center, a point on that surface.

circle graph (*gráfico circular*) A type of graph in which a circle represents the whole. The whole can be divided into sections resembling pieces of a pie, which represent parts of the whole. Therefore, it is also known as a *pie chart*.

circumference (*la circunferencia*) The distance around a circle, given by $C = \pi d$ or $C = 2\pi r$.

classify triangles (*clasificar triángulos*) To group triangles by their attributes. For example, a triangle is isosceles if only two of its sides and angles are equal.

closed figure (*una figura cerada*) A flat figure or shape in which the beginning and end points touch. There are no line breaks or missing sides on a closed figure. Circles, squares, and rectangles are examples of closed figures.

coefficient (*el coeficiente*) A constant used as a factor in an algebraic expression. In the expression $2x + 3y$, the coefficient of x is 2 and the coefficient of y is 3.

coin (*una moneda*) Pennies, nickels, dimes, and quarters are examples of coins.

combine like terms (*combinar términos semejantes*) To gather together and then add or subtract terms with the same variables and the same powers of those variables. For example, $4x^2$ and $-3x^2$ are like terms which, when combined, equal x^2.

commission (*comisión*) A fee or payment paid to a salesperson as a result of a sale of a product or service. The commission is usually a percentage of the total sale price.

common denominators (*los denominadores communes*) Two or more denominators that are the same. For example, $\frac{4}{9}$ and $\frac{8}{9}$ share a common denominator, 9. These are also called *like denominators*.

common factor (*el factor común*) A number that divides evenly into two or more numbers. For example, 7 is a common factor of 21 and 35 because $21 \div 7 = 3$ and $35 \div 7 = 5$.

common multiple (*el múltiplo común*) A number that is a multiple of 2 or more numbers. For example, 24 is a common multiple of 8 and 12 because $8 \times 3 = 24$ and $12 \times 2 = 24$.

commutative property of addition (*la propiedad comutativa de adición*) The order in which numbers are added does not change their sum. For example, $3 + 5 = 5 + 3$.

commutative property of multiplication (*la propiedad comutativa de la multiplicación*) The order in which numbers are multiplied does not change their product. For example, $3 \times 5 = 5 \times 3$.

compare a number (*comparer un númera*) To judge the size of a number or object as it relates to the size of another number or object.

compare unit prices (*comparar precios por unidad*) To compare the cost of one item to the cost of another item.

compass (*el compás*) A tool used to construct circles and arcs.

compatible numbers (*los números compatibles*) Pairs of numbers that are easy to compute mentally. For example, when adding $7 + 22 + 3$, add compatible numbers $7 + 3$ first because the sum is easy to compute.

complementary angles (*unos ángulos complementarios*) A pair of angles whose sum measures 90°. For example, in the diagram, $\angle 1$ and $\angle 2$ are complementary angles.

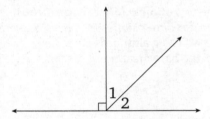

compose a number (*componer un número*) To form a number by adding other numbers. For example, 10 can be composed of 5 and 5, 6 and 4, 7 and 3, etc.

composite number (*un número compuesto*) An integer greater than 1 with more than two factors. For example, 10 is a composite number because its factors are 1, 2, 5, and 10.

compound event (*un evento compuesto*) An event in a probability experiment which involves two or more activities, such as rolling a six-sided number cube and tossing a coin.

conclusion (*una conclusion*) A statement which represents the result or outcome of a problem or experiment.

cone (*un cono*) A solid with a circular base whose surface converges to a point not on the base.

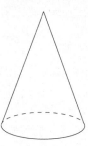

congruent (*congruente*) Having the same shape and the same size. The two squares shown below are congruent.

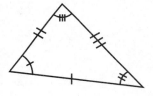

The two triangles shown below are congruent.

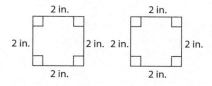

consecutive integers (*unos números enteros consecutivos*) Integers that follow in a sequence in which each number increases by one.

constant (*un constante*) A number or symbol representing a value that does not change. For example, 5 is a constant because its value always stays the same.

construction (*la construcción*) The drawing of a geometric figure such as a circle, arc, angle bisector, or perpendicular bisector, created with tools such as a compass, ruler, or protractor.

convert (*converter*) To express a given measurement in terms of a different unit of measurement. For example, 2 yards can be converted to feet using the fact that 1 yard equals 3 feet. Therefore, 2 yards equals 6 feet.

coordinate geometry (*la geometría de coordenadas*) The study of geometric figures such as points, lines, and polygons, as well as the properties of these figures in the context of the coordinate grid. The coordinate grid consists of a horizontal line (*x*-axis) and a vertical line (*y*-axis), which are labeled with numbers at even intervals.

coordinate plane (*el sistema de coordenadas plano*) A plane formed by a horizontal line (*x*-axis) and a vertical line (*y*-axis). The plane is divided into four quadrants in which ordered pairs, or points, are plotted.

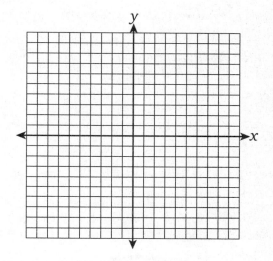

corresponding angles (*unos ángulos correspondientes*) Angles that are in the same position in two or more similar polygons are corresponding and equal. For example, $\angle A$ and $\angle B$ are corresponding angles in the similar triangles shown below.

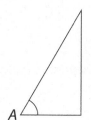 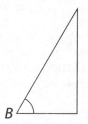

corresponding sides (*unos lados correspondientes*) In similar polygons, sides in the same position are corresponding and proportional. For example, $\overline{AB}$ and $\overline{DE}$ are corresponding sides.

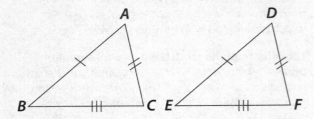

counting numbers (*números naturals*) The set of numbers used for counting (1, 2, 3, …).

cube (*un cubo*) A rectangular prism with six square sides equal in size and shape.

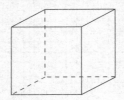

cup (*una taza*) A unit of volume in the customary measurement system, abbreviated as "c". One cup equals 8 fluid ounces.

currency symbols (*los símbolos de moneda*) Symbols used to label amounts of money. In the United States, the symbol $ represents dollars and the symbol ¢ represents cents.

customary measurement system (*el sistema de medición acostumbrada*) The system of measurement used in the United States.

customary units of measure (*las unidades de la medición acostumbradas*) The units used to measure length, distance, volume, and weight in the United States. The basic units include the foot, cup, and pound.

cylinder (*un cilindro*) A solid with two equal and parallel circular bases.

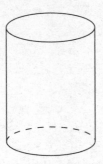

D

data (*los datos*) Information about a situation, group, or event.

day (*un día*) A twenty-four-hour period starting at 12:00 midnight and ending the following midnight.

decagon (*un decágono*) A 10-sided polygon.

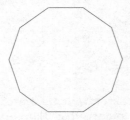

decimal fraction (*una fracción decimal*) A fraction with a power of ten (10, 100, 1,000, etc.) as the denominator. For example, 0.06 can be written as $\frac{6}{100}$. This is a decimal fraction because the denominator (100) is a power of 10.

decimal number (*un número decimal*) A number containing a decimal point. For example, 0.25 is a decimal number read as *twenty-five hundredths*.

decimal point (*una coma decimal*) The point in a decimal number which separates the whole numbers (to the left of the point) and the decimal fractions (to the right of the point). For example, the number 24.55 represents 24 whole units and fifty-five hundredths of another unit.

decimeter (*el decímetro*) A unit of length in the metric system, abbreviated as "dm". There are 10 decimeters in 1 meter.

degree measure of an angle (*una medida del grado de un ángulo*) A measure of the size of an angle. A circle, or one complete turn, measures 360°.

degree of a polynomial (*grado de polinomio*) The largest exponent of the polynomial's terms. For example, the degree of $(x^3 + 2x^2 - x + 4)$ is 3.

denominator (*un denominador*) The number below the division line in a fraction. It represents the number of equal parts into which the whole or group is divided. For example, in the fraction $\frac{3}{5}$, the denominator is 5.

density (*la densidad*) The ratio of the mass of an object to its volume.

dependent events (*un evento dependiente*) Two or more events in which the outcome of any one event affects the outcome of any of the other events.

develop formulas (*desarrollar fórmulas*) To create an algebraic rule for calculating a number. For example, the rule or formula for calculating the circumference of a circle is $C = \pi d$.

diameter (*el diámetro*) A line segment connecting two points on a circle and passing through the center of the circle. The length of the diameter is equal to twice the length of the radius. In the diagram, $\overline{AB}$ is the diameter of the circle.

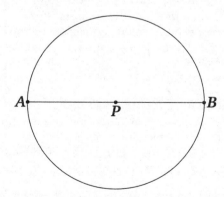

difference (*la diferencia*) The result of subtracting two numbers.

digit (*un dígito*) Any of the numerals 0 to 9.

digital clock (*un reloj digital*) A timepiece that shows time without hour and minute hands.

dilate (*dilatar*) To transform a figure by enlarging or reducing it.

dimensions (*dimensiones*) The measures of an object's sides or altitude—most commonly length, width, and height.

distance (*la distancia*) The measurement between two points in a plane.

distributive property (*la propiedad distributiva*) The product of a factor and a sum or difference is equal to the sum or difference of the products. For example, $3(5 + 6) = 3(5) + 3(6)$.

divide (*divider*) To break a whole into parts.

dividend (*un dividendo*) The total amount you are dividing. In the example, $6 \div 3 = 2$, 6 is the dividend.

divisible (*divisible*) A number is divisible by another number when the division leaves a remainder of zero.

division (*division*) An operation that divides a whole or set into equal parts. It is performed on two numbers to get a third number called the *quotient*.

divisor (*un divisor*) The amount by which you are dividing. In the example $8 \div 4 = 2$, 4 is the divisor.

dollar (*el dólar*) The basic unit of paper money used in the United States. One dollar is equal to 100 cents.

domain (*el dominio*) The set of all possible values for the unknown in an open sentence. In addition, the domain is also the set of all possible values for the independent variable in an algebraic equation.

double (*duplicar*) To multiply by two.

double-bar graph (*una gráfica de barras dobles*) A bar graph that compares two sets of data.

double-line graph (*una gráfica de líneas dobles*) A line graph that compares two sets of data.

E

edge (*el borde*): The line along which two sides of a solid figure meet.

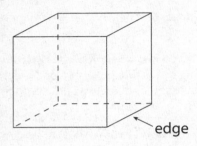

edge

elapsed time (*el tiempo transcurrido*): The amount of time that passes between the beginning and end of an event.

endpoint (*el término*) The starting or ending point of a line segment.

equal (*igual a*) Two numbers or expressions are equal if they have the same value. For example, $3 + 2 = 4 + 1$.

equation (*una ecuación*) A math sentence that uses an equal sign to show that two quantities have the same value.

equation of a line (*una ecuación de una línea*) A mathematical statement containing an equal sign that represents a set of points that form a straight path extending forever in both directions.

equidistant (*equidistante*) Two points are equidistant from a line if the distances from each point to the line are equal.

equilateral triangle (*un triángulo equilateral*) A triangle with three equal sides and three equal angles. Each of the angles in an equilateral triangle measures 60°.

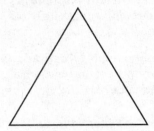

equivalent (*equivalente*) Two numbers or expressions are equivalent if they have the same value. For example, $6 + 6$ and $10 + 2$ are equivalent because both are equal to 12.

equivalent decimals (*unos decimales equivalentes*) Two decimals are equivalent if they have the same value. For example, 0.2 and 0.20 are equivalent because when written as fractions, $\frac{2}{10}$ and $\frac{20}{100}$, they can both be simplified to $\frac{1}{5}$ and therefore are equal in value.

equivalent fractions (*unas fracciones equivalentes*) Fractions that, when simplified to lowest terms, are exactly equal to one another. For example, $\frac{2}{4}$ and $\frac{8}{16}$ are equivalent fractions because both simplify to $\frac{1}{2}$.

equivalent numerical expressions (*unas expresiones numéricas equivalentes*) Two numbers or expressions are equivalent if they have the same value. For example, 2×2 and $3 + 1$ are equivalent numerical expressions because $2 \times 2 = 4$ and $3 + 1 = 4$.

equivalent units (*unidades equivalentes*) Measurements which are equal in size even though they are measured in different units. For example, 12 inches is the same as 1 foot and 1 milliliter is the same as 1 cubic centimeter.

estimate (*estimar*) A result close to the exact result, that is found by approximating or rounding the numbers given in the problem.

estimation strategies (*estrategias de estimar*)
Methods used to arrive at an approximate answer to a problem. For example, rounding numbers is one way to estimate the answer to a problem.

evaluate (*evaluar*) To use the order of operations to determine the value of an expression. For example, you can evaluate the expression $(5 + 3) \times 2$ by following the order of operations to get $8 \times 2 = 16$.

even number (*un número par*) A number that is divisible by 2. Even numbers end in 0, 2, 4, 6, or 8.

event (*el evento*) An action performed during a probability experiment. For example, rolling a six-sided number cube and tossing a coin are examples of events in a probability experiment.

exchange rate table (*tabla de tasas de cambio*) A chart which lists the value of a country's currency (money) compared to the value of other countries' currencies.

expanded form (*la forma extendida*) The expanded form of a number shows the parts of that number broken down by place value. For example, the expanded form of 3,425 is $3,000 + 400 + 20 + 5$.

expenses (*los gastos / costos*) The total amount of money spent, including all costs.

experimental results (*los resultados experimentales*) The recorded outcomes of an experiment in which a test is performed on one or more groups of subjects.

exponent (*el exponente*) A number written above and to the right of a base that tells how many times the base is to be used as a factor. For example, the expression $3 \times 3 \times 3 \times 3$ is written as 3^4 because the base is used 4 times.

exponential form (*la forma exponencial*) A way to write numbers using exponents. For example, 2^5 is written in exponential form.

extend a pattern (*continuar una configuración*) To continue a given sequence or design by using the rule established in it. For example, the extension of the sequence 2, 4, 6, 8 is 10, 12, 14, 16.

exterior angle (*ángulo externo*) An angle on the outside of a polygon formed by one side of the polygon and the extension of a second side of the polygon. The angles formed outside of parallel lines cut by a transversal are also called *exterior angles*. For example, in the figure below, $\angle Y$ is an exterior angle.

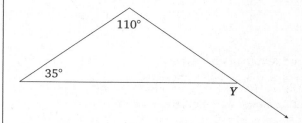

extremes of a proportion (*extremos de una proporción*) In a proportion, the numerator of the first fraction and the denominator of the second fraction are called the *extremes*. For example, in the proportion $\frac{2}{3} = \frac{6}{9}$, the extremes are 2 and 9.

F

face (*la cara*) A flat side of a solid figure.

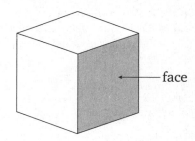

face

factor (noun) (*un factor*) Any of two or more quantities that are multiplied together. In the number sentence $3 \times 11 = 33$, the factors are 3 and 11.

factor (verb) (*descomponer en factores*) To write a number or expression as a product of its factors. For example, 14 can be factored as 2×7.

Fahrenheit (*grado Fahrenheit*) A scale for measuring temperature. Degrees Fahrenheit is written using the symbol °F. Water freezes at 32°F and boils at 212°F.

favorable outcomes (*resultados favorables*)
An outcome that is expected or hoped for as a result of an experiment.

fifths (*quintos*) One or more of five equal parts of a whole.

fixed distance (*distancia fija*) A distance or amount of space that remains the same.

foot (*un pie*) A unit of length in the customary measurement system, abbreviated as "ft". One foot equals 12 inches.

formula (*una formula*) A rule that describes how to calculate a certain quantity or measurement. For example, the formula for the area of a rectangle is $A = l \cdot w$, where A represents the area, l represents the length, and w represents the width.

formulate conclusions from graphs (*hacer conclusiones de una gráfica*) To summarize information from the data shown in a graph.

formulate predictions from graphs (*hacer predicciones de una gráfica*) To guess or estimate future data by extending a pattern shown in a graph.

four-digit number (*un número de cuatro dígitos*) A number containing 4 numerals, each of which can range from 0–9. For example, 2,367 is a four-digit number.

fourths (*los cuartos*) One or more of four equal parts of a whole.

fraction (*una fracción*) A number in the form $\frac{numerator}{denominator}$, where the numerator and denominator are whole numbers and the denominator is not zero. Fractions are used to represent parts of a whole object or part of a collection of objects. For example, $\frac{1}{3}$ is a fraction that represents one out of three equal parts of a whole.

frequency (*frecuencia*) The number of times an event occurs in a specified amount of time.

frequency table (*tabla de frecuencia*) A table showing the number of times an event (or several events) occurred in specified amounts of time.

front-end estimation (*la estimación frontal*) A way of estimating the solution to a problem by rounding each number to its largest place value and then mentally calculating the answer. For example, to mentally estimate 6,432 + 2,297, round the numbers to 6,000 + 2,000 to get 8,000.

function (*función*) A mathematical relationship between two sets of numbers in which each element of the first set (the domain) is matched with exactly one element of the second set (the range).

function notation (*notación de función*) The line $y = 2x + 1$ can be written using function notation as $f(x) = 2x + 1$. The notation $f(x)$ means that the function has an input of x.

function rule (*regla de función*) A mathematical relationship between two sets of numbers expressed using function notation, where each element of the first set (the domain) is matched with exactly one element of the second set (the range). For example, $f(x) = 3x$ is a function rule.

Fundamental Counting Principle (*el principio fundamental de contar*) If one event has p possible outcomes, and an independent event has q possible outcomes, then the first event followed by the second event has $p \cdot q$ possible outcomes.

G

gallon (*un galón*) A unit of volume in the customary measurement system, abbreviated as "gal". A gallon is equal to 4 quarts.

geometric figure (*una figura geométrica*) Any shape consisting of a set of points. For example, a line, line segment, plane, triangle, rectangle, cube, and sphere are all geometric figures.

geometric pattern (*una configuración geométrica*) A design created using shapes (such as lines, squares, circles, triangles, and rectangles).

geometry (*la geometría*) The study of points, lines, angles, planes, shapes, and solids.

gram (*un gramo*) The basic unit of weight in the metric system, abbreviated as "g".

graphically (*gráficamente*) A geometric object can be described graphically by drawing it on a coordinate grid.

gratuity (tip) (*propina*) An amount of money (a percentage of the total bill) given to a person as an extra payment for good service. For example, waiters, hair stylists, and cab drivers generally receive gratuities.

greater than (*más de*) A number is greater than another number if its value is larger. For example, 200 > 150 because 200 has a larger value than 150.

greatest common divisor, GCD (*el máximo divisor en común*) The largest number that divides evenly into two or more other numbers. For example, the greatest common divisor of 18 and 27 is 9. (Also known as the greatest common factor.)

greatest common factor, GCF (*el máximo factor en común*) The largest number that is a factor of two or more numbers. For example, the greatest common factor of 18 and 27 is 9. (Also known as the greatest common divisor.)

H

half hour (*media hora*) A unit of time equal to 30 minutes.

halves (*las mitades*) One of two equal parts of a whole.

halving (*partir en dos*) To divide a number, object, or group of objects into two equal parts.

height (*la altura*) The distance between the top and the bottom of an object. The height of a prism or cylinder is the perpendicular distance between the bases.

heptagon (*un heptágono*) A seven-sided polygon.

hexagon (*un hexágono*) A six-sided polygon.

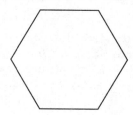

histogram (*un histograma*) A bar graph with no spaces between the bars. The bars represent the frequency of data over a specific interval.

hour (*la hora*) A unit of time equal to 60 minutes.

hundred chart (*un cuadro de gráficos de cien*) A 10 × 10 table labeled 1 through 100 used to learn counting to 100, skip counting, and number patterns.

hundred thousands (*cien miles*) Any of the first nine multiples of the number 100,000.

hundreds (*cientos/as*) Any of the first nine multiples of the number 100.

hundreds place (*el valor posicional de los cien*) A place value in the base-ten number system that represents the number of 100s that are in a number. It is located three places to the left of the decimal point.

hundredths (*centésimo*) A place value in the base-ten number system representing an amount of $\frac{1}{100}$s in a number. It is located two places to the right of the decimal point.

hypotenuse (*la hipotenusa*) The longest side of a right triangle. It is the side opposite the right angle in a right triangle.

I

identity element for multiplication (*el elemento de identidad para la multiplicación*) The number 1, because no matter what number it is multiplied by, it always results in that number. For example, $1 \times 7 = 7$.

identity property of addition (*la propiedad de identidad de la adición*) The sum of any number and 0 is that number. For example, $4 + 0 = 4$. The number 0 is called the *additive identity*.

identity property of multiplication (*la propiedad de identidad de la multiplicación*) The product of any real number and 1 is that number. For example, $9 \times 1 = 9$. The number 1 is called the *multiplicative identity*.

image (*imagen*) The resulting figure after a transformation has been performed.

impossible outcomes (*resultados imposibles*) Outcomes of an experiment that cannot happen. For example, when testing probability by rolling a six-sided number cube labelled 1 through 6, rolling a 7 is an impossible outcome.

improper fraction (*una fracción impropia*) A fraction in which the numerator is larger than the denominator and the denominator is not zero. For example, $\frac{6}{5}$ is an improper fraction.

inch (*una pulgada*) A unit of length in the customary measurement system, abbreviated as "in." Twelve inches equal one foot.

income (*ingreso*) Money received from a salary or investment.

inequality (*una inecuación*) A math sentence that uses symbols such as $>$ (greater than) and $<$ (less than) to compare values. For example, $10 > 7$ is an inequality.

input values (*el valor puesto*) An input value is a number that is put into a number sentence to produce another number (output value). For example, the input value 4 can be put into the number sentence $m = n + 2$ for n to get $m = 4 + 2$. Therefore, $m = 6$ is the output value.

integer (*número entero*) One of the set of whole numbers and their opposites. Zero is also an integer, and is neither positive nor negative. The set below is the set of all integers.

$$\{\ldots -3, -2, -1, 0, 1, 2, 3,\ldots\}$$

integer coefficients (*coeficientes enteros*) Integers used as factors in an algebraic expression. In the expression $4a + 6b$, the integer coefficient of a is 4 and the integer coefficient of b is 6.

integral (*números enteros*) Relating to integers (positive and negative whole numbers and zero) and not fractional parts.

integral exponent (*potencias de números enteros*) An exponent or power which is an integer (one of the set of whole numbers and their opposites and zero). For example, in the expression 5^2, 2 is the integral exponent.

interest (*el interés*) Payment for the use of borrowed money, usually in the case of savings or loans. Simple interest (compounded at intervals) is calculated using the formula $I = Prt$, where P is the amount of principal (the original amount borrowed), r is the interest rate per unit of time, and t is the amount of time.

interest rate (*tasas de interés*) The percentage of the principal (the original amount borrowed) paid for the use of borrowed money.

interior angles (*unos ángulos interiores*) Angles on the inside of a polygon formed by two connecting sides of the polygon.

interpret graphs (*interpretar gráficos*) To summarize the results or trends displayed in a graph (line graph, bar graph, circle graph, etc.).

intersecting lines (*lineas que se crucen*) Two lines that intersect at a point.

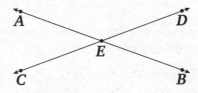

inverse (*el inverso*) A number which, when added to or multiplied by another number, produces 0 (the additive identity) or 1 (the multiplicative identity), respectively. For example, the additive inverse of 5 is −5 because $5 + (−5) = 0$. The multiplicative inverse of 5 is $\frac{1}{5}$ because $5 \cdot \frac{1}{5} = 1$.

inverse operations (*las operaciones inversas*) Operations that are opposites. Addition is the inverse operation of subtraction, and multiplication is the inverse operation of division.

inverse property of addition (*la propiedad inversa de adición*) The sum of a number and its opposite is zero. For example, $5 + (−5) = 0$.

inverse property of multiplication (*la propiedad inversa de multiplicación*) The product of a number and its reciprocal is 1. For example, the reciprocal of 3 is $\frac{1}{3}$. Therefore, $3 \times \frac{1}{3} = 1$.

irrational numbers (*números irracionales*) An irrational number is a real number that cannot be represented as an exact ratio of two integers. Examples include π and $\sqrt{2}$.

irregular polygon (*un polígono irregular*) A polygon that does not have equal sides and equal angles.

isosceles triangle (*un triángulo isósceles*) A triangle with exactly two equal sides and two equal angles.

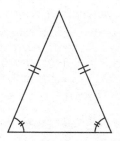

J

justify (*justificar*) To validate the reasoning for a mathematical statement or argument using theorems and mathematical properties.

K

key to a graph (*la clave de una gráfica*) A small area near a graph which explains the meanings of the symbols or markings on that graph.

kilogram (*el kilogramo*) A unit of mass in the metric system, abbreviated as "kg". One kilogram equals 1,000 grams.

kilometer (*el kilómetro*) A unit of length in the metric system, abbreviated as "km". One kilometer equals 1,000 meters.

L

law of exponents for division (*la ley de exponentes para la división*) To divide two powers that have the same base, subtract the denominator's exponent from the numerator's exponent. The difference is the new exponent for the shared base. For example, $\frac{4^5}{4^3} = 4^2$.

law of exponents for multiplication (*la ley de los exponentes para la multiplicación*) To multiply two powers that have the same base, add the exponents. For example, $3^2 \cdot 3^4 = 3^6$. To find the power of a power, multiply exponents. For example, $(5^2)^4 = 5^8$. To find the power of a product, find the power of each factor and multiply. For example, $(2 \cdot 3)^6 = 2^6 \cdot 3^6$.

least common denominator, LCD (*el denominador común más bajo*) The smallest number that is a multiple of the denominators of 2 or more fractions. For example, the least common denominator of $\frac{3}{4}$ and $\frac{1}{6}$ is 12 because 12 is the smallest number that is a multiple of both 4 and 6.

least common multiple, LCM (*el múltiplo común más bajo*) The smallest number that is a multiple of two or more numbers. For example, the least common multiple of 6 and 8 is 24.

legs of a right triangle (*las bases / los catetos de un triángulo recto*) The two sides that intersect to form the right angle in a right triangle.

length (*la longitud*) The distance across a line segment or a side of a polygon.

less than (*menos de*) A number is less than another number if its value is smaller. For example, $85 < 99$ because 85 has a smaller value than 99.

levels of precision (*los niveles de precisión*) The degree to which a measurement is exact and accurate. Measurements in smaller units have higher levels of precision. For example, when measuring the length of a paper clip, a measurement in millimeters will be more precise than a measurement in centimeters or inches.

like denominators (*los denominadores communes*) Two or more denominators that are the same. For example, $\frac{4}{9}$ and $\frac{8}{9}$ share a like denominator, which is 9. (Also known as the *common denominator*.)

like terms (*terminos semejantes*) Terms with the same variables and the same powers. For example, $4x^2$ and $-3x^2$ are like terms.

line (*una línea*) An infinite set of points that form a straight path extending forever in both directions.

linear equation (*una ecuación lineal*) An equation that represents a straight line and can be written in the form $ax + by = c$.

linear inequalities (*desigualdades lineales*) A mathematical statement that can be written in one of four ways: $ax + by > c$, $ax + by < c$, $ax + by \geq c$, and $ax + by \leq c$.

linear relationship (*la relación lineal*) Pairs of numbers have a linear relationship if they form a straight line on a coordinate grid.

line graph (*una gráfica de línea*) A graph that uses lines or line segments to indicate relationships among data.

line of symmetry (*la línea de simetría*) A line of symmetry divides a figure so that when the image is folded along the line, the two sides match exactly.

line segment (*un segmento de una línea*) A set of points that forms a straight path with two endpoints.

line symmetry (*la simetría lineal*) A figure has line symmetry if it can be folded along a line to make two congruent figures.

liter (*el litro*) The basic unit of volume in the metric system, abbreviated as "L".

lowest terms (*los términos más bajos*) When the numerator and denominator of a fraction have no factors greater than 1 in common. For example, $\frac{8}{12}$ written in lowest terms is $\frac{2}{3}$ because both numerator and denominator can be divided by 4. The fraction $\frac{3}{8}$ is already in lowest terms. (Also known as *simplest form*.)

M

magnitude (*la magnitud*) The absolute value of a number.

map scale (*escala de un mapa*) An area on a map which provides a ratio of the distance on the map to the actual distance. For example, a map can be drawn so that each centimeter represents 1 mile.

mass (*la masa*) The amount of matter that an object contains.

mathematical statement (*una enunciado matemática*) An expression or number sentence that may contain numbers, variables, operation symbols ($+$, $-$, $\div$, $\times$), or an equal sign or inequality symbol ($<$, $>$, $\leq$, or $\geq$).

mean of a data set (*la media aritmética*) The average of a set of numbers. The mean is found by dividing the sum of the set by the amount of numbers in the set. For example, to find the mean of {3, 4, 5}, first find the sum by adding $3 + 4 + 5$ to get 12. Then, divide 12 by 3 (the amount of numbers added together) to get a mean of 4. The mean is a measure of central tendency.

means of a proportion (*la media aritmética de una proporción*) In a proportion, the denominator of the first fraction and the numerator of the second fraction are called the *means*. For example, in the proportion $\frac{2}{3} = \frac{6}{9}$, the means are 3 and 6.

measure (*medir*) To obtain the quantity, length, weight, or volume of an object (or set of objects) or liquid.

measurement (*una medida*) The quantity, length, weight, or volume of an object (or set of objects) or liquid.

measures of central tendency (*las medidas de tendencia central*) The measures of central tendency are the mean, median, mode, and range. They help describe the center of a set of data.

median (*mediana*) The number in the middle of an ordered set of numbers. The median of a set with an even number of elements is the arithmetic mean of the two middle elements. The median is a measure of central tendency.

mental math (*el cálculo mental*) A calculation done without pencil, paper, calculator, or computer.

meter (*un metro*) A unit of length in the metric system, abbreviated as "m". One meter equals 100 centimeters.

metric system (*el sistema métrico*) A system of measurement that is based on units of 10.

metric units of capacity (*unidades métricas de capapcidad*) Units of volume in the metric system such as liters, milliliters, and cubic centimeters.

metric units of mass (*la unidad métrica de masa*) Units of weight in the metric system such as grams and kilograms.

metric units of measure (*las unidades de medida métricas*) The units of measure based on units of 10. The basic units of the metric system are the meter, liter, and gram.

mile (*una milla*) A unit of distance in the customary measurement system. One mile equals 5,280 feet.

milliliter (*un mililitro*) A unit of volume in the metric system, abbreviated as "mL". One liter equals 1,000 milliliters.

millimeter (*un milímetro*) A unit of length in the metric system, abbreviated as "mm". One meter equals 1,000 millimeters.

millions (*los millones*) Any of the first nine multiples of the number 1,000,000, which equals $1,000 \times 1,000$.

minute (*un minuto*) A unit of time equal to 60 seconds. There are 60 minutes in one hour.

misleading (*engañoso*) False or deceptive. Statistical data can be misleading when, for example, the x-axis and y-axis are not scaled evenly or completely.

mixed number (*un número mixto*) A number that is comprised of a whole number and a fraction. For example, $4\frac{1}{2}$ is a mixed number.

mode (*el valor que ocurre con mayor frecuencia*) The number that occurs most often in a set of numbers. A set can have more than one mode. The mode is a measure of central tendency.

monomial (*un monomio*) A single term that is made up of a number (also called a *constant*), a variable, or a product of numbers and variables. For example, 4, $2x$, and $-5x^2y^3$ are monomials. Monomials are also called *terms*.

multiple (*un múltiplo*) The product of a given integer and a counting number. For example, the number 3 has multiples such as 3, 6, 9, 12, 15, 18, etc.

multiplicand (*un multiplicando*) The number being multiplied in a multiplication problem.

multiplication (*multiplicación*) An operation on two numbers, called *factors*, to obtain a third number called the *product*. For example, multiplying 4×6 yields 24.

multiplicative inverse (reciprocal) (*inverso multiplicativo / recíproco*) The multiplicative inverse of a number x is $\frac{1}{x}$ because $\frac{x \cdot 1}{x} = 1$, the multiplicative identity. For example, the multiplicative inverse of 5 is $\frac{1}{5}$ and the multiplicative inverse of $\frac{2}{3}$ is $\frac{3}{2}$.

multiplier (*un multiplicador*) The number by which another number is multiplied in a multiplication problem.

multiply (*multiplicar*) To perform an operation on two numbers, called *factors*, to obtain a third number called the *product*. For example, to multiply two numbers such as 7 and 3, you write $7 \times 3 = 21$.

N

negative (*negativo*) Having a value that is less than zero.

nonadjacent side of a triangle (*el lado no adyacente de un triángulo*) Each angle in a triangle has one nonadjacent side. The nonadjacent side has no contact with the angle, and therefore, must lie opposite the angle. In the diagram, the right angle in the triangle has one nonadjacent side, which is the hypotenuse.

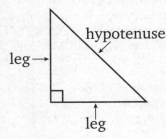

nonagon (*un nonágono*) A nine-sided polygon.

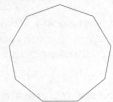

nonlinear equation (*ecuación no linear*) An equation that represents anything other than a straight line. For example, equations representing parabolas and circles are nonlinear equations.

nonlinear relationship (*relación no linear*) Pairs of numbers represent a nonlinear relationship if they do not form a straight line on a coordinate grid.

non-perfect squares (*cuadros imperfectos*) Numbers whose square roots are not integers. For example, 5 is a non-perfect square because $\sqrt{5}$ is not an integer. Non-perfect squares are also irrational numbers.

non-repeating decimal (*decimales que no repiten*) A decimal number with digits that never enter into a repeating pattern. For example, $\pi = 3.14159265\ldots$. Its digit pattern never repeats, and therefore, it is a non-repeating decimal. Non-repeating decimals are irrational numbers.

nonstandard measure (*una medida no estándar*) A measurement found using unusual units of measure such as paper clips, sticks of gum, shoes, etc.

non-terminating decimal (*decimal infinito*) A decimal number that continues forever with no ending digit. For example, the fraction $\frac{1}{3}$ written as a decimal is $0.3333\ldots$ and is a non-terminating decimal. However, non-repeating decimals can also be non-terminating (e.g., $\pi = 3.14159265\ldots$). Therefore, non-terminating decimals can be rational or irrational numbers.

not equal to (*desigual a*) Two numbers or expressions are not equal to each other if they do not have the same value. For example, $3 \neq 5$ means 3 is not equal to 5.

not preserved (*no preservado*) If two figures are similar, then their measurements are said to be preserved. If two figures are not similar, then their measurements are not preserved.

number (*un número*) A digit or series of digits representing a certain numeric value.

number line (*la línea de números*) A line on which points are marked off at regular intervals (i.e., evenly spaced) and labeled with ordered numbers.

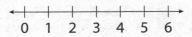

number sentence (*una frase de números*) A true numeric statement containing numbers, operation symbols, and either $>$, $<$, $\geq$, $\leq$, , or $=$. For example, $3 + 6 = 9$, $7 > 1 + 3$, or $\frac{3}{5} + \frac{1}{5} = \frac{4}{5}$.

number system (*el sistema de numeración*) A way of representing and counting numbers. For example, the decimal system represents numbers using a decimal point and place values such as ones, tens, and hundreds.

numeral (*el numeral*) Any digit from 0–9.

numeration (*la numeración*) The counting of numbers.

numerator (*un numerador*) The number above the division line in a fraction. It represents the number of equal parts being described. For example, in the fraction $\frac{3}{5}$, 3 is the numerator and it represents three out of five equal parts.

numeric expression (*una expresión numérica*) A math phrase that contains numbers and operation symbols, but no variables or relation symbols. For example, $3 \times 6 + 9$ is a numeric expression.

numeric patterns (*unas configuraciones numéricas*) A repeating rule in a group of numbers. For example, in the group of numbers 4, 8, 12, 16, 20, the pattern is "add 4."

numerical problems (*unos problemas numéricos*) A math problem that contains numbers and operation symbols.

numerically (*numéricamente*) A problem is expressed numerically if it contains numbers and operation symbols such as $+$, $-$, $\div$, and $\times$.

obtuse angle (*el ángulo obtuso*) An angle whose measure is between 90° and 180°.

obtuse triangle (*el triángulo obtuso*) A triangle with one angle greater than 90°.

octagon (*el octágono*) An eight-sided polygon.

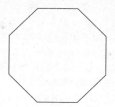

odd number (*los números impares*) An integer that ends in 1, 3, 5, 7, or 9.

ones (*unos*) One represents an individual unit equal in value to the number 1.

ones place (*el valor posicional de uno*) A place value in the base-ten number system that represents the number of 1s that are in a number. It is located one place to the left of the decimal point.

open figure (*una figura abierta*) A figure in which the beginning and end points do not touch.

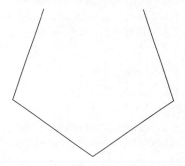

open sentence (*una frase numérica abierta*) A number sentence containing one or more variables. For example, $x + 6 = 8$.

operation (*la operación*) A process performed on numbers. The basic operations are addition, subtraction, multiplication, and division.

operations with polynomials (*operaciones con polinomios*) Polynomials can be added and subtracted by combining like terms. They can also be multiplied using the distributive property and divided using long division.

order (*ordenar*) To put in a sequence from least to greatest or from greatest to least.

order of operations (*el orden de operaciones*)
A rule indicating the order in which operations should be performed in an expression. Perform operations inside parentheses first, then simplify exponents. Next, perform multiplication and division from left to right, and finally, perform addition and subtraction from left to right.

ordered pair (*par ordenado*) A pair of numbers (*x*, *y*) that can be graphed on a coordinate grid. The variable *x* represents the value along the *x*-axis and the variable *y* represents the value along the *y*-axis.

organized chart (*una carta organizada*) A chart used to put information into categories using rows and columns.

organized list (*una lista organizada*) A list of numbers or other information arranged in categories or columns.

ounce (*una onza*) A unit of weight in the customary measurement system, abbreviated as "oz". There are 16 ounces in one pound. It can also refer to a unit of volume. Eight fluid ounces equal one cup.

P

parallel lines (*las líneas paralelas*) Two different lines in the same plane which never intersect.

parallelogram (*el paralelogramo*) A four-sided polygon with opposite sides parallel and equal.

part (*la parte*) A section of a whole.

pattern (*una configuración*) Regularity in a situation, nature, an event, a design, or in a set of numbers (e.g., spirals on pineapples, designs in quilts, the number sequence 3, 6, 9, 12,…).

pentagon (*un pentágono*) A five-sided polygon.

percent (*por ciento*) A ratio that compares a number to 100. The symbol for percent is %. For example, 50% means 50 out of 100, and 35% means 35 out of 100.

percent decrease (*disminución porcentual*) The percent that represents the ratio of the amount of decrease to the original amount $\left(\frac{\text{amount of decrease}}{\text{original amount}}\right)$.

percent increase (*incremento porcentual*) The percent that represents the ratio of the amount of increase to the original amount $\left(\frac{\text{amount of increase}}{\text{original amount}}\right)$.

percent of quantity (*el por ciento de una cantidad*) A part, per hundred, of a whole amount. For example, 50% of 10 is the same as $\frac{50}{100} \times 10$, which equals 5.

perfect square (*cuadro perfecto*) A number whose square root is an integer. For example, since $\sqrt{4} = 2$ and $\sqrt{9} = 3$, 4 and 9 are perfect squares.

perimeter (*el perímetro*) The distance around a polygon. This distance can be found by adding the lengths of all the sides.

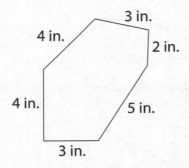

perimeter = 21 in.

perpendicular bisector (*bisectriz perpendicular*) A ray, line, or line segment that is perpendicular to and also bisects another line segment.

perpendicular lines (*unas líneas perpendiculares*) Lines that intersect to form right angles.

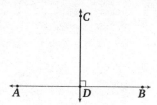

personal references (*unas referencias personales*) The use of personal measurements, such as arm length or hand length to measure an object. For example, a hand is approximately 6 inches. Therefore, if a desk is 7 hands long then it is $7 \times 6 = 42$ inches long.

pi (π) A number which represents the ratio of a circle's circumference to its diameter. It is an irrational number that is approximately equal to 3.14159.

picture graph (*un pictograma*) A graph in which pictures are used to represent values.

pint (*una pinta*) A measure of volume, abbreviated as "pt". Two cups equal 1 pint; 2 pints equal 1 quart.

place value (*el valor posicional*) The value of a digit depending on its position in a number. In the numeral 5,270, the 2 is in the hundreds place, which gives it a value of 200.

plane figure (*una figura plana*) A figure that lies in only one plane. Circles, squares, rectangles, and parallelograms are examples of plane figures.

plot (*trazar*) To graph ordered pairs (x, y) on the coordinate plane.

point (*el punto*) A location in space represented by a dot. The point is the basis for building all other figures, such as line segments, circles, squares, etc.

poll (*una encuesta*) To ask a group of people the same question or set of questions with the goal of organizing and analyzing the answers.

polygon (*un polígono*) A figure with three or more sides in which each side is a line segment. For example, squares, rectangles, parallelograms, and trapezoids are polygons.

polynomial (*un polinómico*) A mathematical expression that contains one or more monomials. For example, $(16y^4 + 1)$ and $(2x^3y + 8y - 4)$ are polynomials.

population (*la población*) In statistics, the entire group about which a researcher will draw conclusions. Examples of populations include: black bears in North America, students in mathematics classes in Michigan, and women under the age of 40.

positive (*positivo*) Having a value that is greater than zero.

possible outcomes (*unos resultados posibles*) The possible results of an experiment. For example, when rolling a six-sided number cube, the possible outcomes are 1, 2, 3, 4, 5, and 6.

post meridian, P.M. (*después del mediodía*) The label given to the hours between 12:00 noon and 12:00 midnight.

pound (*una libra*) A unit of weight in the customary measurement system, abbreviated as "lb". One pound equals 16 ounces. Two thousand pounds equal one ton.

power (*la potencia*) A number written above and to the right of a base that tells how many times the base is to be used as a factor. For example, the number 4 raised to the fifth power is written as 4^5. It represents $4 \times 4 \times 4 \times 4 \times 4$. The term *power* is also used to describe a value written in exponential form.

prediction (*una predicción*) An educated guess about the outcome of an event or several events. For example, when tossing a coin 10 times, a prediction could be that the coin will land on heads 5 times.

pre-image (*imagen preliminar*) The name of a figure before it has been transformed.

preserved (*preservado*) If two figures are similar, then their measurements are said to be preserved. If two figures are not similar, then their measurements are not preserved.

prime factorization (*descomposición en factores primos*) The expression of a composite number as the product of its prime factors. For example, the prime factorization of 315 is $3^2 \times 5 \times 7$.

prime number (*un número primo*) A whole number greater than one that has only two factors: 1 and itself. For example, 2, 3, 5, 7, and 11 are prime numbers.

prism (*una prisma*) A solid formed by four or more flat sides that intersect with bases. For example, a rectangular prism is shown below.

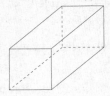

probability (*la probabilidad*) The likelihood or chance of an event occurring, expressed as a number from 0 to 1. A probability of 1 means that the event is certain to occur, while a probability of 0 means that the event cannot occur.

product (*el producto*) The solution to a multiplication problem. For example, in the number sentence $3 \times 5 = 15$, the product is 15.

profit (*ganancia*) A measurement of revenue minus expenses.

proper fraction (*una fracción propia*) A fraction in which the numerator is smaller than the denominator. For example, $\frac{5}{8}$ is a proper fraction.

properties of real numbers (*propiedades de numeros reales*) The commutative, associative, distributive, inverse, and identity properties. These properties apply to all real numbers.

property (*la propiedad*) A rule used to simplify expressions. For example, the commutative property states that the order in which numbers are added does not change the sum: $4 + 2 = 2 + 4$.

proportion (*la proporción*) An equation stating that two ratios are equivalent.

proportional reasoning (*la razonamiento proporcional*) Reasoning used to understand the relationship between two ratios and to solve for a missing component of a proportion.

protractor (*un transportador*) A tool used to measure angles in degrees.

pyramid (*un pirámide*) A solid with a polygon as a base and triangles for faces that meet at a point on top.

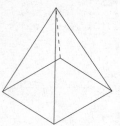

Pythagorean theorem (*el teorema pitagórico*) The sum of the squares of the lengths of the legs in a right triangle is equal to the square of the length of the hypotenuse. In a right triangle with a and b as the lengths of the legs and c as the length of the hypotenuse, the relationship can be expressed as $a^2 + b^2 = c^2$.

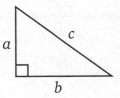

Q

quadrant (*un cuadrante*) One of the four sections of a coordinate plane.

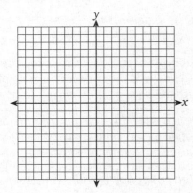

quadratic equation (*la ecuación cuadrática*) An equation that contains a polynomial of degree 2 that has at most two solutions. Quadratic equations can be written in the form $ax^2 + bx + c = d$.

quadrilateral (*un cuadrilátero*) A four-sided polygon.

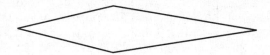

quart (*un cuarto*) A unit of liquid measure, abbreviated as "qt". Two pints equal one quart, and 4 quarts equal 1 gallon.

quotient (*un cociente*) The answer when dividing a number by another number. For example, in the number sentence $6 \div 3 = 2$, the quotient is 2.

R

radius (*el radio*) A line segment connecting a point on a circle with the center of the circle. The radius is half the length of the diameter. In the figure, $\overline{PA}$ is the radius of the circle.

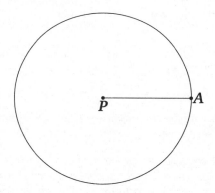

range (*el rango*) In statistics, the difference between the greatest and the smallest values in a set of data. The range can also refer to the set of output values for a function, or the set of dependent values.

rate (*tasa*) A comparison of two quantities that have different units of measure; for example, miles per hour, cans per dollar, miles per gallon, and dollars per pound.

rate of change (*tasa de cambio*) The amount of change in one variable with respect to another variable.

rate of interest (*tasa de interés*) The percentage of the principal paid for the use of borrowed money.

ratio (*una proporción*) A comparison of two numbers, often written as a fraction. For example, if there are three boys in class for every two girls, the ratio of boys to girls is $\frac{3}{2}$ or 3:2 (read as "3 to 2").

rational numbers (*números racionales*) Numbers that can be expressed as the quotient of two integers; for example, $\frac{7}{3}$, $\frac{5}{11}$, $-\frac{5}{13}$, 7, and $\sqrt{16}$ are all rational numbers.

ray (*un rayo*) A part of a line that extends from a given point in one direction only.

real numbers (*números reales*) The set of all rational and irrational numbers.

reasonable estimate (*unas estimaciones razonables*) A guess at an answer that is within the range of possible answers.

reasonableness (*carácter razonable*) The quality of an answer that is not extreme or excessive.

record data (*documentar datos*) To document the information gathered throughout a study or experiment in an organized way.

rectangle (*el rectángulo*) A four-sided polygon in which opposite sides are parallel, and there are four right angles.

rectangular prism (*prisma rectangular*) A three-dimensional figure whose sides are all rectangles; a box.

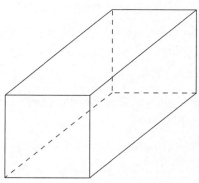

reflect (*reflejar*) To transform a figure by flipping it across a fixed line, resulting in a mirror image.

regroup (*reagrupar*) To reorganize the values in a number to carry out addition and subtraction.

Subtraction with regrouping:

$$\begin{array}{r} \overset{3\ 10}{7\cancel{4}0} \\ -\ 519 \\ \hline 221 \end{array}$$

regular polygon (*un polígono regular*) A closed, two-dimensional figure in which all sides and angles are congruent. For example, a square is a regular polygon.

related facts (*los hechos relacionados*) Information that is needed to solve a problem.

relation (*la relación*) A mathematical relationship between two sets of numbers.

relative error (*error relativo*) In measurement, the relative error is the discrepancy between the measured result and the accepted value of the measurement, usually expressed as a percent.

remainder (*el resto*) A whole number that is left over after one whole number is divided by another. For example, when dividing 8 by 6, the answer is 1 with a remainder of 2.

repeating decimal (*un decimal periódico*) A decimal with a block of one or more digits that repeats without end. The fraction $\frac{2}{11}$ (which is equal to 0.1818181818…) can be expressed as the repeating decimal $0.\overline{18}$.

rhombus (*un rombo*) A four-sided polygon in which the opposite sides are parallel, and all four sides are equal.

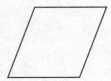

right angle (*un ángulo recto*) An angle that measures exactly 90°.

rotate (*rotar*) To transform a figure by turning it around a fixed point.

rotational symmetry (*la simetría rotatoria*) A two-dimensional figure has rotational symmetry if a point exists about which the figure can be rotated less than a full 360° turn, so that the image of the rotation matches the original figure exactly. This point is called the *center of rotation*. For example, the letters S, I, X, and H have rotational symmetry, while A, C, W, and L do not.

rounding (*redondear un número*) An action that changes a number to a more convenient value. For example, to round to the nearest hundred, find the hundred that is closest to the given number; that is, 4,295 rounded to the nearest hundred is 4,300.

rule (*una regla*) A sequence of steps that can be used to solve a problem or perform an action on a number.

ruler (*una regla*) A tool used to measure the length of objects in inches or in centimeters.

S

sale price (*el precio rebajado / precio de venta*) The price of an item after a discount has been taken.

sales (*ventas / ofertas*) Promotions at stores which offer discounts on merchandise. Sales can also refer to the total amount of money collected for goods or services for a specified period of time. For example, Paul's total in sales for the month of June was $595.00.

sample space (*las posibilidades*) The set of all possible outcomes of an experiment.

sampling (*un muestreo*) A group of individuals or individual circumstances that are representative of the whole, which can be studied to determine information about the entire population.

scale on a graph (*la escala de una gráfica*) The labeled numbers that increase by equal amounts on the *x*- and *y*-axes.

scale to measure mass (*la balanza*) An tool used to determine the weight of an object.

scalene triangle (*un triángulo escaleno*) A triangle that does not have any equal sides or angles.

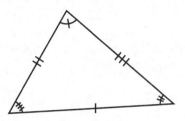

scientific notation (*la notación científica*) A shorthand way of writing very large or very small numbers. A number expressed in scientific notation is expressed as a decimal greater than or equal to 1 and less than 10, multiplied by a power of 10 (e.g., $7,000 = 7 \times 10^3$ and $0.0000019 = 1.9 \times 10^{-6}$).

second (*un segundo*) A unit of time. Sixty seconds equal one minute.

sector (*un sector*) A portion of a circle in the shape of a "pie piece." It is enclosed by two radii and an arc.

segment bisector (*un bisectriz de un segmento*) A point, line segment, or plane which divides a line segment into two congruent line segments.

set of data (*un colección de datos*) A collection of numbers or information about objects or events.

set of objects (*un colección de objetos*) A collection of shapes or entities.

shape (*una figura*) A closed figure in space. Squares, circles, triangles, rhombi, and rectangles are all examples of shapes.

side (*un lado*) One of the line segments that make up a polygon.

similar figures (*unas figuras similares*) Figures that have the same shape but not necessarily the same size. All corresponding angles are equal, and all corresponding sides are proportional.

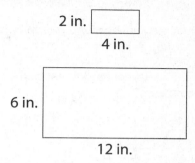

similar triangles (*unos triángulos similares*) Triangles that have the same shape but not necessarily the same size.

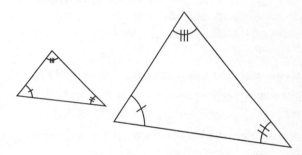

simple interest (*interés simple*) Payment for the use of borrowed money, usually in the case of savings or loans. Simple interest (compounded at intervals) is calculated using the formula $I = Prt$, where P is the amount of principal (the original amount borrowed), r is the interest rate per unit of time, and t is the amount of time.

simplest form (*los términos más bajos*) When the numerator and denominator have no factors greater than 1 in common. For example, $\frac{8}{12}$ written in simplest form is $\frac{2}{3}$ because both the numerator and the denominator can be divided by 4. The fraction $\frac{3}{8}$ is already in simplest form, also known as *lowest terms*.

simplify (*simplificar*) To use operations and/or combine like terms in order to write an expression in simplest form.

simplify expressions (*simplificar expresiones*) To combine like terms in order to write expressions in simplest form.

simplify fractions (*simplificar fracciones*) To write a fraction in simplest form (see definition above).

single event (*un evento singular*) One of a set of tests performed during a probability experiment.

single-event experiment (*un experimiento de un evento singular*) An experiment whose outcome is determined by one occurrence or event. For example, a single-event experiment could involve tossing a coin once.

sixths (*los sextos*) One or more of six equal parts of a whole.

skip-count (*contar saltando unos numeros*) Counting by multiples of a number. For example, skip-counting by 2s gives the sequence 2, 4, 6, 8,... and skip-counting by 5s gives 5, 10, 15, 20,....

slope (*pendiente de una línea*) The ratio of the change in *y* to the corresponding change in *x*, expressed as the constant *m* in the linear function equation $y = mx + b$. Graphically, the slope can be described as $\frac{\text{rise}}{\text{run}}$.

slope-intercept form (*forma pendiente-intercepción*) A linear equation of the form $y = mx + b$, where *m* is the slope and *b* is the *y*-intercept.

solid figure (*una figura sólida*) A three-dimensional figure with length, width, and height such as a cube, cylinder, or pyramid.

solution (*la solución*) A value or mathematical representation that satisfies the conditions of a problem.

solution set (*conjunto de soluciones*) The set of all possible values of a variable, which satisfy the conditions of a problem.

solution set of an equation (*un conjunto de soluciones de una ecuación*) The set of all possible values of a variable, which satisfy an equation.

solution set of an inequality (*un conjunto de soluciones de una desigualdad*) The set of all possible values of a variable, which satisfy an inequality.

solve (*solucionar*) To determine the answer to a problem.

spatial reasoning (*el razonamiento espacial*) The ability to mentally visualize and manipulate spatial figures and patterns.

sphere (*una esfera*) The set of all points in a space that are the same distance from a given point in that space, called the *center*.

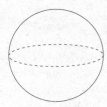

square (*un cuadro*) A four-sided polygon with four equal sides and four equal angles.

square root (*la raíz cuadrada*) One of two equal factors of a number. Geometrically, the square root is the length of the side of a square that has an area equal to the number for which the square root is being found. For example, $\sqrt{16} = 4$, because a square with an area of 16 square units has sides measuring 4 units each in length. The symbol for square root is $\sqrt{\ }$.

standard form of a number (*una forma estándar de un número*) The way in which numbers are usually written. For example, in the equation $3^2 = 9$, 9 is written in standard form and 3^2 is written in exponential form.

standard measure (*las unidades de la medida estándar*) The customary units of measure used in the United States. The basic units include the foot, cup, and pound.

statistics (*estadísticas*) The study of collecting, organizing, and interpreting data.

straight angle (*un ángulo recto*) An angle with a measure of exactly 180°.

subset (*subconjunto*) A set of elements entirely contained within a larger set of elements. For example, the set of all even numbers is a subset of the set of all real numbers.

substitute (*sustituir*) To replace an unknown in a number sentence with a number.

subtract (*sustraer*) To take away one number from another. To subtract, the sign − is used. For example, $6 - 4 = 2$.

subtraction (*sustracción*) The process of taking away a number from another number. To subtract, the sign − is used. For example, $6 - 4 = 2$.

sum (*la suma*) The result of adding two or more numbers.

supplementary angles (*los ángulos suplementarios*) A pair of angles whose sum measures 180°. For example, in the diagram, ∠1 and ∠2 are supplementary angles.

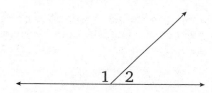

surface area (*área de superficie*) The area of the faces or outside surfaces of a three-dimensional figure.

survey (*una encuesta*) An interview of a group to find information such as likes, dislikes, needs, and wants.

symbols in verbal form (*los símbolos en forma verbal*) Ways of representing numbers and objects that are written on paper or spoken in words. For example, the expression "$m + 7$" means "7 more than m."

symbols in written form (*los símbolos en forma escrita*) Ways of representing numbers and objects on paper without using numbers. For example, a variable such as n is an example of a symbol that can be written to represent an unknown number.

symmetry (*la simetría*) A geometric figure has line symmetry if it can be divided into two congruent sections that are mirror images of each other. In addition, a geometric figure has rotational symmetry if a point exists about which the figure can be rotated less than a full 360° turn so that the image of the rotation matches the original figure exactly. For example, the letters S, I, X, and H have rotational symmetry, while A, C, W, and L do not.

system of equations (*un sistema de ecuaciones*) A number of equations with an equal number of variables.

$$\begin{cases} 2x - y = 1 \\ -4x + 9y = 5 \end{cases}$$

The brace indicates that the system of equations is to be solved simultaneously.

system of inequalities (*un sistema de desigualdades*) A number of inequalities with an equal number of variables.

$$\begin{cases} 2x - y < 1 \\ -4x + 9y \geq 5 \end{cases}$$

The brace indicates that the system of inequalities is to be solved simultaneously.

T

table (*una tabla*) A display of information organized into rows and columns so that the data can be easily read and understood.

table of values (*tabla de valores*) A display of numbers or other data arranged in rows and columns in which the facts can be easily read and understood.

tax (*impuestos*) A fee paid for purchasing goods or services. It is usually a percentage of the total cost of the purchase.

ten thousands (*diez milésimos*) Any of the first nine multiples of 10,000, which equals 100×100.

tens (*decenas*) Any of the first nine multiples of the number 10.

tens place (*el valor posicional de los diez*) A place value in the base-ten number system that represents the number of 10s that are in a number. It is located two places to the left of the decimal point.

GLOSSARY

tenths (*décimos*) One or more of ten equal parts of a whole.

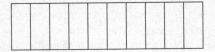

term (*un término*) The part of a variable expression that is separated from other terms (or monomials) by addition or subtraction symbols. It can be a number, variable, or the product of numbers and variables. In the sum $a + b$, a and b are the terms.

terminating decimal (*un decimal finito*) A decimal that ends. The fraction $\frac{3}{4}$ can be expressed as the terminating decimal 0.75. Terminating decimals are rational numbers.

thirds (*terceros*) One or more of three equal parts of a whole.

thousands (*miles*) Any of the first nine multiples of the number 1,000, which equals 100×10.

thousandths (*millares*) Any of the first nine multiples of the number $\frac{1}{1,000}$.

three-digit number (*un número tridigital*) A number containing 3 numerals, each of which can range from 0–9. For example, 455 is a three-digit number.

three-dimensional figure (*una figura tridimensional*) A figure in space that has a height, width, and depth.

time (*el tiempo*) A system of keeping track of the minutes and hours in a day. There are 24 hours in one day and 60 minutes in each hour.

ton (*una tonelada*) A unit of weight in the customary measurement system. One ton equals 2,000 pounds.

transformation (*transformación*) A movement of a figure that does not change the angles of the figure and preserves the proportions of the side lengths.

transformational geometry (*la geometría transformacional*) The study of the manipulations of geometric figures, such as rotations, reflections, dilations, and translations.

translate (*trasladar*) To move a figure to a new position without turning or flipping the figure.

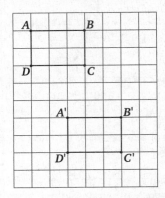

transversal (*transversal*) A line that intersects two or more lines in the same plane.

trapezoid (*un trapezoide*) A four-sided polygon with exactly one pair of parallel sides. The parallel sides are called the *bases*.

triangle (*el triángulo*) A three-sided polygon. The sum of the interior angles of a triangle is 180°.

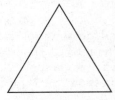

trinomial (*un trinomio*) A polynomial that consists of three terms, or monomials, when written in standard form. For example, $4n^3 + 8n - 6$ is a trinomial.

two-dimensional figure (*una figura de dos dimensiones*) A figure in a plane which has a length and a width.

U

unit fraction (*una fracción unitaria*) A fraction with 1 as a numerator and any integer as the denominator. For example, $\frac{1}{4}$ is a unit fraction.

unlike denominators (*unos denominadores desemejantes*) Denominators of two or more fractions that are not the same. For example, $\frac{2}{5}$ and $\frac{7}{8}$ have unlike denominators, namely 5 and 8.

V

validity of sample methods (*la validez de los métodos de muestra*) The degree to which the sampling (selection of individuals or individual circumstances to study) is fair, impartial, and representative of the population being studied.

value (*el valor*) The numeric worth of a digit, variable, or expression.

variable (*una variable*) An unknown quantity. A variable may be represented by a letter.

Venn diagram (*diagrama de Venn*) A visual picture used to represent the relationships among sets. For example, the Venn diagram below represents the number of students involved in different after-school activities. The sections where the circles overlap represent students involved in more than one activity.

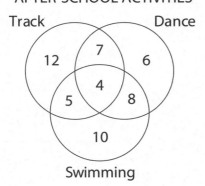

AFTER-SCHOOL ACTIVITIES

verbal expression (*una expresión verbal*) A combination of numbers, variables, and operations written or spoken in words. For example, "James found 3 more than 2 times as many seashells as Jorge."

verbal form (*la forma verbal*) Using written or spoken words. An example of a mathematical statement in verbal form is "James has 3 times as many musical instruments as Kenneth."

verbal sentence (*una frase verbal*) A sentence written or spoken in words.

vertex (*el vértice*) The point shared by two rays or line segments forming an angle. It can also refer to the point at which two lines intersect or three faces of a rectangular prism meet.

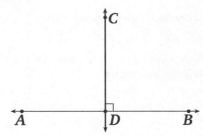

vertical (*vertical*) Being in an upright position. A vertical line runs up and down and is perpendicular to a horizontal line. In the diagram, $\overline{CD}$ is a vertical line segment.

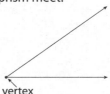

vertical angles (*ángulos opuestos por el vértice*) Pairs of opposite congruent angles formed by intersecting lines. In the diagram, $\angle AED$ and $\angle CEB$ are vertical angles.

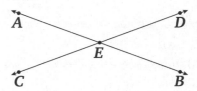

vertical line test (*prueba de una linea vertical*)
A rule used to determine if a graph represents a function. The rule states that if no vertical line can be drawn anywhere through the graph so that the line intersects more than one point on the graph, then the graph represents a function.

vertical lines (*líneas verticales*) Lines which are in an upright position. Vertical lines run up and down and are perpendicular to horizontal lines. In the diagram, $\overline{CD}$ is a vertical line.

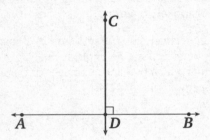

vertices (*los vértices*) The plural of *vertex* (see page 335).

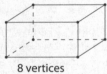

8 vertices

visualization (*la visualización*) Imagining or picturing an object, shape, or situation in your mind.

volume (*volumen*) The number of cubic units inside a three-dimensional figure.

W

week (*la semana*) A unit of time equal to 7 days.

whole (*entero*) The sum of all the parts of a number or object.

whole number (*un número entero*) Any of the set of numbers {0, 1, 2, 3, 4,…}.

whole unit (*una unidad entera*) A number or object not divided into parts.

width (*la anchura*) A dimension of a rectangle, usually the shorter side.

written symbols (*símbolos escritos*) Letters, words, or other symbols which are written to represent other values, such as numbers.

Y

yard (*una yarda*) A unit of length in the customary measurement system, abbreviated as "yd". One yard is equal to three feet.

y-intercept (*intercepción y*) The *y*-coordinate at which a graph crosses (or intercepts) the *y*-axis. A line can be identified by its slope and *y*-intercept in slope-intercept form, $y = mx + b$.

Z

zero property of addition (*la propiedad de cero de adición*) The sum of 0 and any number is that number. For example, $0 + 5 = 5$.

zero property of multiplication (*la propiedad de cero de multiplicación*) When multiplying any number by 0, the answer is 0. For example, $9 \times 0 = 0$.